...ed
...ls,
...l.

...r
...s
...or
...ence and a passion for travel.

**Rely on Thomas Cook as your
travelling companion on your next trip
and benefit from our unique heritage.**

Thomas Cook **pocket** guides

BARCELONA

Thomas
Cook

Your travelling companion since 1873

Written by Teresa Fisher
Updated by Nadia Feddo

Published by Thomas Cook Publishing
A division of Thomas Cook Tour Operations Limited
Company registration No: 3772199 England
The Thomas Cook Business Park, 9 Coningsby Road
Peterborough PE3 8SB, United Kingdom
Email: books@thomascook.com, Tel: +44 (0)1733 416477
www.thomascookpublishing.com

Produced by The Content Works Ltd
Aston Court, Kingsmead Business Park, Frederick Place
High Wycombe, Bucks HP11 1LA
www.thecontentworks.com

Series design based on an original concept by Studio 183 Limited

ISBN: 978-1-84848-284-5

First edition © 2006 Thomas Cook Publishing
This third edition © 2010 Thomas Cook Publishing
Text © Thomas Cook Publishing
Maps © Thomas Cook Publishing/PCGraphics (UK) Limited
Transport map © Communicarta Limited

Series Editor: Lucy Armstrong
Production/DTP: Steven Collins

Printed and bound in Spain by GraphyCems

Cover photography (Detail in Park Güell) © Gregory Wrona/Alamy

CONTENTS

SYMBOLS KEY

The following symbols are used throughout this book:

ⓐ address ⓣ telephone ⓦ website address ⓛ opening times
ⓝ public transport connections ⓘ important

The following symbols are used on the maps:

𝓲 information office		▪ points of interest	
✈ airport		○ city	
✚ hospital		○ large town	
⛊ police station		○ small town	
⊟ bus station		═ motorway	
⊟ railway station		─ main road	
Ⓜ metro		─ minor road	
✝ cathedral		─ railway	
❶ numbers denote featured cafés & restaurants			

Hotels and restaurants are graded by approximate price as follows:
£ budget price **££** mid-range price **£££** expensive

Abbreviations used in addresses:

Av. Avinguda
C/ Carrer
Pl. Plaça

▶ *La Sagrada Familia – a work in progress*

INTRODUCING
Barcelona

Introduction

Barcelona is one of the great Mediterranean cities. Dynamic, stylish and innovative, the capital of Catalonia boasts sun, sea, sandy beaches and some of the finest and most eccentric art and architecture in the world. Its unique urban landscape resembles a living museum. Even today, the city is a Mecca for the world's top architects, from local stars like Ricardo Bofill to international names such as Richard Rogers and Jean Nouvel, and their avant-garde structures sit comfortably alongside Gothic churches and dazzling *Modernista* edifices – the hallmark of the city.

It would be easy to spend a week simply paying homage to Barcelona's *Modernista* treasures, in particular those of its most famous son Antoni Gaudí. Throughout the world, people have marvelled at the creations and drawn inspiration from this great master. But the city abounds in sights and attractions that will appeal to all tastes, pockets and ages, including some of the finest galleries and museums in Europe. Barcelona is also home to La Rambla, one of the world's most famous boulevards. This is the street everyone visits, talks about and tries to photograph or paint. It is more theatre than thoroughfare but it is nonetheless a vital part of the city's makeup – this is where Barcelona's heart beats loudest.

A massive facelift prior to the 1992 Olympics converted the previously run-down, old city into a chic, cosmopolitan metropolis bursting with pride and self-confidence. The transformation of the derelict seafront rejuvenated the city, reminding the Barcelonans of their maritime heyday, and giving rise to the slogan *Barcelona oberta al mar* (Barcelona open to the sea). Subsequent coastline projects included events such as the 2004 Forum of Cultures, which provided a vast new entertainment and leisure area at the northeastern end of the city; and the Hotel Vela, a sail-shaped luxury hotel and leisure complex which helped to sex up the rather dilapidated old fishing docks of the Barceloneta. Now Barcelona is considered the 'style capital of Europe', exuberant and sophisticated, with world-class shopping, an exceptional cultural scene and a flamboyant nightlife. Remember, this is the European city that never sleeps – tonight doesn't usually start until tomorrow.

Today, Barcelona continues to reinvent itself district by district, celebrating its past by restoring its old buildings, while at the same time remaining at the forefront of contemporary culture. It is the richest, fastest-growing, most creative and most stylish city in Spain – and what's more, its motto is *Barcelona Es Teva* (Barcelona belongs to you).

⬤ *A view of the city from La Sagrada Família*

When to go

SEASONS & CLIMATE

Barcelona has no low season as there are always things going on. The best time to visit, however, is late spring/early summer, when the weather is warm but not too hot, and the street life is at its most vibrant.

The coldest season is winter, with an average temperature of 10°C (54°F). Snow is rare and days are generally mild but damp, with the occasional day of clear blue skies and bright crisp sunshine.

In spring the average temperature is around 15°C (59°F). These are some of the wettest months but, from late March onwards, the weather starts to warm up. After Easter, outdoor café tables become more popular and by May it is usually warm enough to eat alfresco in the evenings.

During summer, the average temperature is around 25°C (75°F), but it can reach 37°C (99°F) in July and August when the humidity can make the city feel oppressively hot and muggy. Although there is little rain, the occasional sudden violent thunderstorm provides a brief but refreshing respite from the heat.

Early autumn is also an ideal time to visit, with generally mild sunny weather. The average autumn temperatures are around 16°C (53°F). By mid-October, the fine weather becomes more intermittent, with frequent heavy rainfalls, and the pavement tables disappear until spring.

ANNUAL EVENTS

Throughout the year, religious processions, festivals and traditions turn the city of Barcelona into an open-air theatre. Here are some of the highlights.

January

Any Nou (New Year) Barcelonans eat 12 grapes for luck to the chimes of midnight. The *Reis Mags* (Wise Men) arrive by boat to tour the city on 5 January, showering the crowd with sweets. Children traditionally receive their Christmas presents now, or lumps of sugar coal if they've misbehaved.

February

Festival de Santa Eulàlia On 12 February, the feast day of St Eulàlia is celebrated with a week of traditional parades, *gegants* (giant figures), concerts, *sardanes* (Catalan folk dances) and *castellers* (human castles). Many events are focused on children.

⬤ *Gaudí's rippling* trencadís *benches in Park Güell*

Carnestoltes A week of colourful pre-Lenten parades ends on Ash Wednesday with the symbolic burial of a sardine on Barceloneta beach. Many events take place in nearby Sitges.

March–May

Setmana Santa Easter sees church services and processions throughout the city, particularly by the Gothic cathedral on Palm Sunday; godparents buy godchildren a *mona*, or elaborate chocolate sculpture.

Sant Jordi (St George; 23 Apr) This local alternative to St Valentine's Day is when sweethearts exchange gifts – traditionally a rose for the woman and a book for the man. La Rambla becomes a huge outdoor bookshop.

Corpus Christi Traditional *sardanes* dancing outside the cathedral, and the 18th-century tradition of *Ou com Balla* (dancing egg): an empty eggshell balances on the cathedral's fountain to symbolise the Eucharist.

Primavera Sound A three-day music festival in late May filling the vast Parc del Fòrum with enormous crowds and big names from all music genres. Ⓦ www.primaverasound.com

June & July

Sónar A three-day music and multimedia festival. Ⓦ www.sonar.es

Sant Joan Summer solstice bonfires, the *Nit del Foc* (night of fire) in La Barceloneta and all-night beach parties.

De Cajón A new flamenco music festival. Ⓦ www.deflamenco.com

August & September

Festa Major de Gràcia Gràcia's streets compete for the best decorations and entertainment; carrer Verdi is always impressive. The finale sees fireworks and a *correfoc* (fire run) – devils and dragons scattering firecrackers.

La Mercè The city's main week-long fiesta takes place around the 24th September. Events include free concerts, fireworks, an air show, traditional parades and *sardanes* dancing all finished off with the wildest *correfoc* (fire run) of the year.

November & December
Festival Internacional de Jazz One of Europe's most prestigious jazz festivals. ⓦ www.theproject.es
Nadal (Christmas) The Santa Llúcia craft fair is outside the Catedral (2–23 December) and a large nativity scene is set in Plaça Sant Jaume.

PUBLIC HOLIDAYS
New Year's Day 1 Jan
Epiphany 6 Jan
Good Friday 2 Apr 2010, 22 Apr 2011, 6 Apr 2012
Easter Monday 5 Apr 2010, 25 Apr 2011, 9 Apr 2012
May Day 1 May
Whit Monday 24 May 2010, 13 June 2011, 28 May 2012
St John's Day 24 June
Assumption Day 15 Aug
Catalan National Day 11 Sept
La Mercè 24 Sept
Discovery of Americas 12 Oct
All Saints' Day 1 Nov
Constitution Day 6 Dec
Immaculate Conception 8 Dec
Christmas Day 25 Dec
St Stephen's Day 26 Dec

Gaudí & *Modernisme*

The *Modernisme* movement – a taste for what is modern – emerged in Barcelona at the turn of the 19th century with the aim of breaking away from the past through new art forms. It was Spain's home-grown interpretation of art nouveau and, thanks to its greatest exponent, Antoni Gaudí, Catalan *Modernisme* had the greatest impact, influencing all forms of European art, architecture, literature and theatre and making Barcelona a veritable open-air museum of *Modernista* style.

⬤ *The dragon's back and saint's cross at Casa Batlló*

No single architect has ever marked a major city quite as comprehensively and spectacularly as Gaudí did in Barcelona. For many people, Gaudí alone is sufficient reason to visit Barcelona. He designed many of its most characteristic buildings; throughout the city mansions, parks, schools, gateways, lampposts and sculptures provide a constant reminder of his genius. His innovative work represents a flamboyant fusion of structure and decoration, giving precedence to use of

GAUDÍ'S BARCELONA HIGHLIGHTS

Casa Batlló (see page 93)
Park Güell (see page 94)
Palau Güell (see page 107)
La Sagrada Família (see page 96)
Casa Milà 'La Pedrera' (see page 90)

colour and light within architectural forms. His remarkably organic structures are frequently adorned with his trademark pinnacles, towers and rooftop terraces. Particularly striking are Casa Milà (see page 90), with its extraordinary rippling façade devoid of straight lines and right-angled corners, and Casa Batlló (see page 93), an imaginative example of the fusion of architecture with the decorative arts of the époque. The green, blue and ochre mosaics of this enigmatic building symbolise the scaly skin of the dragon, its knobbly roof the dragon's back, the balconies represent the skulls and bones of its victims, while the tower shows St George's cross.

However, Gaudí's most emblematic structure is the still unfinished Temple Expiatori de la Sagrada Família (see page 96), the city's iconic temple that he spent over 40 years creating, personally going out into the street to raise funds among the passers-by to facilitate its construction. 'The patron of this project is not in a hurry' he once remarked. Tragically, in 1926 he was run over by a tram on the Gran Via and died in hospital. When his identity was eventually discovered, Barcelona gave him what was almost a state funeral. His body is fittingly buried in the crypt of the Temple, to which he devoted much of his life.

History

According to legend, Hercules founded Barcelona in 2000 BC on his colonial expedition from Africa aboard nine boats: *barça* (boat), *nona* (nine). In fact, it was the Carthaginians who first established a stronghold here around 230 BC, allegedly naming the city *Barcino* after Hannibal's father, Hamil Barca. The Carthaginians were swiftly followed by the Romans in about 15 BC. However, the rise of Barcelona's fortunes coincided with the decline of the Roman Empire and the invasion of the Visigoths in 531. In 878, Guifré el Pilós (Wilfred 'The Hairy') founded the independent country of Catalonia. He named himself the first Count of Barcelona, thereby founding a dynastic line that was to rule an increasingly powerful nation for several centuries.

During the early Middle Ages, Barcelona flourished during its brief Moorish occupation, until the Christians took Barcelona in 1229 under Catalan King Jaume I. The city became a powerful naval base and trading centre – one of the three most important merchant cities in the Mediterranean, along with Genoa and Venice. The lavish medieval mansions of the old town – former residences of the Counts of Barcelona and the Kings of Catalonia and Aragón – together with such impressive new buildings as the Catedral, the church of Santa Maria del Mar and the Drassanes shipyards, stand as testimony to this golden age. In the 15th century, Catalonia became a self-governing region, and built its own parliament buildings in Barcelona. However, from the 16th to the 18th centuries, as Spain's economic focus turned away from the Mediterranean to the colonisation of the Americas, Barcelona experienced a period of economic decline and, during the Spanish War of Succession, Catalonia lost its autonomous status.

During the 18th century, Catalonia began to re-emerge in what is known as the Catalan *renaixença* (renaissance), thanks to a steady growth in agriculture, textiles, wine production and shipping. The 19th-century industrial revolution created new prosperity in Barcelona, making it the fastest expanding city in Spain. This also brought about a cultural 'renaissance', as Catalan language and literature began to flourish once more.

Hand in hand with the cultural renaissance came the *Modernisme* movement (the Catalan offshoot of art nouveau). Ildefons Cerdà designed the grid-like Eixample district to house the burgeoning middle classes, while *Modernista* architects like Gaudí designed the district's apartment buildings and mansions.

The 20th century brought Barcelona new challenges, including the Franco dictatorship from the end of the Spanish Civil War until 1975, during which time Catalan national identity was repressed. However, the 1992 Olympic Games provided a boost for the city, spurring the transformation of the once down-at-heel waterfront into one of the most chic harbours in Europe. The whole city was radically revamped and the effort continued with subsequent ambitious projects such as the Forum of Cultures.

Today, the city goes from strength to strength, renovating and reinventing itself district by district, with La Ribera, El Born, El Raval and most recently, La Barceloneta, emerging as newly fashionable quarters. Barcelona keeps its reputation as a forward-looking city at the forefront of design and contemporary culture.

Lifestyle

Barcelonans are fiercely proud of their unique Catalan culture and will repeatedly inform you that Catalonia and its capital city are not Spanish. Indeed they will even try to convince you that Barcelona, not Madrid, is Spain's premier city and, in their eyes, it really is.

Their pride in their city and in their regional culture is manifested in every aspect of daily life – in their cuisine (see page 24) and in their language. Although Barcelona still has two official languages, Catalan and Castilian Spanish, *Català* has completely taken over on public signage and is spoken as the everyday language by over a third of the city's population and understood by over 90%. Even the city's celebrated football team, FC Barça, represents so much more than just a football club. During the Franco era, it was a rallying point for Catalans at matches against their arch rivals, Real Madrid, and it became the focus of their hatred of central government. At the height of the dictatorship, match results were pre-ordained so that Madrid would win. Still today, whenever they play Real Madrid, all of Spain is gripped, and should Barça win, the streets of Barcelona erupt to the sound of car horns, fireworks and popping cava corks.

Barcelonans certainly know how to enjoy themselves, and no month goes by without a festival, a fiesta or a public holiday. But they are also hard-working and prosperous. In a recent survey, Barcelona's economic progress was ranked third among cities of the world. Punctuality is important for meetings, and formal wear is the norm. Business hours are generally 08.00 or 09.00 until 18.00 or 19.00, with a lengthy lunch break between 13.30 and 15.30 or 16.00 to include an afternoon siesta during hotter months. These days, more and more companies are switching to a more European 9–5 timetable to facilitate international business.

Barcelonans rarely invite guests into their home. As in many Mediterranean countries, they prefer to socialise in the city's 2,500 bars, cafés and restaurants. Eating is regarded as one of life's great pleasures, and mealtimes are often lengthy gatherings with all the family. And there is no denying that Barcelonans are night owls. The city's intoxicating club scene is among the best (and the latest) in Europe. Here evening begins when most people elsewhere have already gone to bed – clubs rarely open before 3am.

Culture

Barcelona is one of Europe's great cities, thanks mainly to its rich cultural heritage and the dynamism of the contemporary arts and design scene. It is exceptional for the quantity and quality of museums and galleries in proportion to its size – with over 50 to choose from, together with a busy calendar of music and arts events in theatres and concert venues throughout the city, not to mention an impressive range of street artists and entertainers.

Make the informative Museu d'Història de la Ciutat (City History Museum), the lively Museu d'Història de Catalunya (History Museum of Catalonia) or the fascinating Museu Marítim (Maritime Museum) your first port of call. Once you have a grasp of the city's colourful history, walks around town are all the more rewarding. If you intend to visit several museums, it is worth getting a Barcelona Card (valid for two to five days), which offers discounts of 10–100 per cent at the city's main museums, together with free travel on public transport.

The city galleries showcase some dazzling permanent collections by three of the prime movers and shakers in Spanish modern art – Pablo Picasso, Joan Miró and Antoni Tàpies. The Museu Nacional d'Art de Catalunya spans several centuries with its remarkable displays, which include one of the world's most important collections of Romanesque art and an impressive selection of *Modernista objets d'art*, while the Museu d'Art Contemporani de Barcelona contains some striking contemporary art. Art aficionados should buy an Articket, a multi-ticket providing half-price admission to seven of the city's foremost art centres: MNAC, Fundació Joan Miró, Fundació Antoni Tàpies, CCCB, MACBA, La Pedrera and Museu Picasso. The similar Arqueoticket allows unlimited access to five archaeologically-oriented museums.

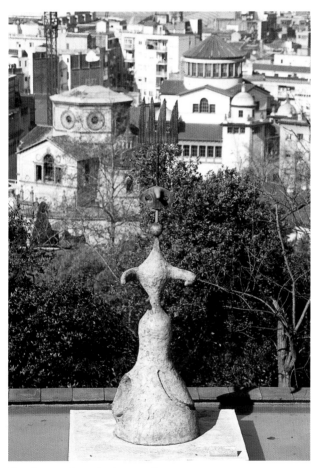

○ *Sculpture at the Fundació Joan Miró*

Barcelona also boasts some of the world's finest and most eccentric architecture. Its extraordinary urban landscape resembles a living museum, from the ancient Gothic quarter, built within the Roman city walls – a honey-coloured maze of dark, narrow alleys and charming, hidden squares – to the regimental grid plan of the turn-of-the-century Eixample district, studded with its many eye-catching jewels of *Modernista* architecture, and beyond to the space-age constructions of more recent years. Tourist offices provide the Ruta del Modernisme guide, covering 115 *Modernista* buildings in Barcelona and Catalonia marked by the small red circles on the pavement outside. Valid for a year, it contains discounts of 15–50 per cent. The Ruta del Disseny guide covers the city's 100 best-designed buildings with nine separate itineraries.

A showcase for the best of Spain's theatrical talent, the city is home to such renowned troupes as Els Comediants, La Fura dels Baus, Els Joglars and Tricicle. It is also famed for its wide diversity of musical events from classical music, opera and ballet through jazz, pop and rock, to some of the most innovative music festivals in Europe. In 1999 the city opened the Auditori arts centre (home to the National Catalan Orchestra) and regained its prestigious opera house, the Gran Teatre del Liceu, whose season runs from October until mid-July, with ballet staged during the summer months. Another major classical music venue, the Palau de la Música Catalana – a *Modernista* gem – is worth visiting whatever the programme.

One of the most important annual musical events is the 'Grec' Summer Festival, staged at the Teatre Grec on Montjuïc hill – an ambitious open-air programme of theatre, music and dance, some in English. Other festivals are devoted to jazz, flamenco and contemporary music.

▶ *Rooftop chimneys at Casa Milà 'La Pedrera'*

MAKING THE MOST OF
Barcelona

Shopping

As a leading European city of fashion and design, Barcelona boasts a wealth of shopping opportunities, from designer boutiques to quirky speciality shops, small district markets to glitzy department stores. It offers a unique shopping experience, cleverly fusing tradition and innovation, and its main interior design stores and small, eccentric boutiques make the hunt for gifts here especially enjoyable.

Best buys include clothing, shoes and decorative goods. Look out for outlets selling clothes by local fashion designers Antoni Miró, Josep Font and Lydia Delgado in particular.

Start your spending spree in the Eixample district, where the grid-like streets are lined with chic interior design shops and prestigious

◆ *The Maremàgnum complex in Port Vell*

fashion emporia. The most exclusive are brilliant for window-shopping, in particular Passeig de Gràcia, La Rambla de Catalunya and the stretch of Avinguda Diagonal between Plaça Joan Carles I and Plaça Francesc Macià.

Old-fashioned arts and crafts shops juxtapose more off-beat boutiques in the intimate streets and alleyways of the Barri Gòtic. Try Carrer Banys Nous for arts and antiques; Carrer Petritxol for art galleries, home accessories and gift ideas; and Avinguda Portal de l'Àngel and Carrer Portaferrissa for high-street fashion chains and shoes.

The newly trendy neighbouring districts of La Ribera and El Born contain myriad tiny craft workshops, jewellers and designer boutiques, as well as some superb art galleries in the streets around Museu Picasso. El Corte Inglés is the city's only real department store, with several different locations (notably Plaça Catalunya, Avinguda Portal de l'Àngel, and Plaça Francesc Macià), and the waterfront also attracts shoppers to the Maremàgnum shopping centre and the new Diagonal Mar mall. The new focus for the shopping spotlight is the futuristic shopping and leisure complex designed by Richard Rogers inside the former Les Arenes bullring in Plaça d'Espanya.

Larger shops tend to open 09.00 to 21.00 Monday–Saturday. Smaller shops close during the siesta (13.00–16.30), early on Saturdays and frequently on Mondays. Some shopping centres (including the Maremàgnum) open on Sundays, and food shops and markets generally open early in the morning. There are 40 covered municipal markets across the districts of the city but the most famous, La Boqueria, is centrally placed on La Rambla and is one of the best places to stock up on picnic supplies or even have a quick tapa or two. The Mercat de la Barceloneta has a solar roof, while the Mercat de Santa Caterina in the Born district is famous for its wavy, mosaic-studded roof designed by Enric Miralles. Both have high-quality restaurants.

Eating & drinking

Don't let Barcelona's dazzling cultural scene divert you from its culinary excellence. The city boasts a huge culture of eating, drinking and conversation, with lengthy lunches and late night dining, and a bewildering choice of eateries from spacious designer brasseries to tiny neighbourhood tapas bars.

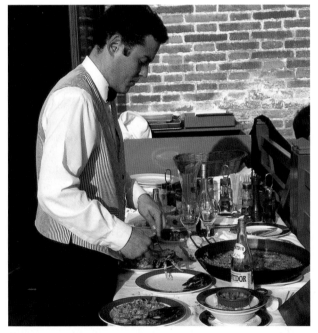

● *Dishing up paella in La Barceloneta*

Barcelonans enjoy good food and often eat out. It is customary in Catalonia to eat late, with lunch served typically from 14.00 to 16.00, aperitifs and tapas in the early evening, then dinner from 21.30 to midnight or later. Many cafés and bars remain open from early morning until late at night. It is advisable to book in most restaurants, especially at weekends. Most offer a fixed price *menú del dia* (fixed lunch menu), which is usually good value but restrictive. The *à la carte* menus generally offer some of the more unusual dishes and regional specialities. Prices on the menu include 7 per cent VAT (*IVA*), unless stated, and it is customary to tip by rounding up the bill after a meal, or to add on 5–10 per cent if you are feeling generous.

There is no such thing as Spanish 'national cuisine' but it is possible to taste various regional styles, including Galician and Basque. The majority of restaurants serve the local cuisine, *la cuina Catalana* – a Mediterranean style of cooking, with bold, sun-drenched flavours in hefty portions.

Traditional Catalan dishes lean heavily on olive oil, tomatoes, garlic, peppers, aubergines, courgettes and herbs which, when mixed, form *samfaina*, a delicious sauce served with meat and fish dishes. Other sauces include *romesco* (nuts, tomatoes and spicy red pepper) and *allioli* (a strong mayonnaise-type blend of garlic and olive oil). Pork is the mainstay of the Catalan diet, although chicken, rabbit, duck, beef and game are popular too. Meats are often cooked

PRICE CATEGORIES
The price guides indicate the approximate cost of a three-course meal for one, excluding drinks.
£ up to €25 ££ €25–50 £££ over €50

with fruit in such delicacies as *pollastre amb pera* (chicken with pears) and *conill amb prunes* (rabbit with prunes). Seafood is hugely popular, from simply grilled sardines to a hearty *sarsuela* (seafood stew). Try the local variant on *paella*, called *fideuà* (using pasta noodles rather than rice) and the eye-catching shellfish platters. Catalan cuisine is unique within Spain for mixing fish and meat together to create such exotic dishes as *sepia amb mandonguilles* (squid with meatballs) and *mar i muntanya* (surf 'n' turf or, literally,

USEFUL DINING PHRASES

I would like a table for ... people
Quisiera una mesa para ... personas
Keyseeyera oona mesa para ... personas

May I have the bill, please?
¿Podría traerme la cuenta,
por favor?
*¿Pordreea trayerme la cwenta,
por fabor?*

Waiter/waitress!
¡Camarero/Camarera!
¡Camareroe/Camarera!

Could I have it well-cooked/medium/rare please?
¿Por favor, la carne bien hecha/al punto/poca hecha?
¿Por fabor, la kahrrne beeyen echa/al poontoh/poka echa?

I am a vegetarian. Does this contain meat?
Soy vegetariano. ¿Lleva carne este plato?
Soy begetahreeahnoh. ¿Yevah carneh esteh plahtoh?

> **TAPAS**
>
> Tapas bars abound throughout the city, serving savoury snacks with a pre-meal drink to *tapar el apetito* (to put a lid on the appetite). If you are overwhelmed by the mouth-watering counter displays, simply point to one or two tempting dishes or order a *tapa combinada* – a bit of everything!

sea and mountain) – a combination of sausages, rabbit, prawns and fish.

The best-known Catalan dessert is *crema catalana* (cream custard topped with caramelised sugar). Look out also for *mel i mató* (fresh cheese with honey); *postre de músic*, simply a handful of mixed nuts and dried fruit with a glass of amaretto; and *coques* (pastries sprinkled with sugar and anything from pine nuts to candied fruit or pork fat).

Don't miss the excellent locally produced wine and sparkling *cava* from the Penedès, Priorat or the Costers del Segre regions.

There are myriad restaurants, tapas bars and other eateries in Barcelona, so it's worth doing some research before setting out in the evening. The Barri Gòtic and Gràcia contain a variety of small, atmospheric restaurants that are generally reasonably priced. Eateries on La Rambla tend to be overpriced and touristy. The Eixample is generally more upmarket and contains many of the city's most vanguard restaurants, and there are plenty of intimate candlelit bistros and fashionable brasseries to be found in La Ribera, El Born and, increasingly, in El Raval. For seafood, head to the Olympic Port or to the atmospheric fishing district of La Barceloneta.

Entertainment & nightlife

Barcelona is a city of night owls, and the vibrant club scene is among the best in Europe. There is plenty to choose from every night, and weekends here start on Thursday. A typical evening begins around 20.30 with tapas and aperitifs in a local bar, followed by a leisurely dinner around 22.30. The usual starting time for opera, ballet and concerts is around 21.00, or 22.00 for theatre. After midnight, music bars become crowded. Around 03.00 the clubs and discos fill up and the famous Barcelonan night movement sweeps across the city until dawn. For those who just don't want to stop, there are 'afters' bars that take the party all the way to lunchtime the next day.

The main nightlife areas are El Born and La Ribera, with their many small bars, and the chic nightspots of L'Eixample. However, the Barri Gòtic and El Raval are also lively and some of the more exclusive bars and clubs are further afield – on Montjuïc hill and the lower slopes of Tibidabo.

The city's flamboyant club scene caters to all tastes, although house and electronic beats take centre stage at present. Many of the clubs are on the European circuit for celebrated DJs and live bands, and there is even an annual Sónar festival of experimental electronic music and technology in June, attracting all the big names in digital sound. During summer the beachfront clubs often have outdoor dancing, and some inland clubs have fantastic dance terraces, some with swimming pools. There are also numerous Latin clubs featuring salsa, merengue and samba beats. Entry to the top clubs is not cheap, so look out for free entry passes at various bars around the city centre or discount flyers, which are sometimes handed out on La Rambla at night. The city also boasts numerous live music venues, ranging from vast rock and pop arenas to traditional flamenco clubs and mellow, intimate jazz bars featuring artists from all over the world.

There's a wide-ranging programme of classical music, ballet and dance, staged in such impressive venues as the beautiful *Modernista* Palau de la Música Catalana and the Gran Teatre del Liceu. Throughout the year, recitals are staged in churches, museums and monasteries, and during summer months in some of the city parks, including Ciutadella Park, Park Güell and the Teatre Grec on Montjuïc hill,

◯ *A tempting display at one of Barcelona's many tapas bars*

which stages an open-air summer festival of theatre, music and dance. Barcelona's theatre programme is unlikely to appeal to visitors, unless you speak Catalan or Spanish, in which case there is the full spectrum from classical to avant-garde on offer.

Several cinemas show screenings in the original version with subtitles, including the Boliche, Casablanca-Gràcia, Verdi and the Yelmo Icària Cineplex. Look for VO (*versió original*) in the listings.

BARS & CLUBS

The best source of local entertainment listings is the magazine *Guía del Ocio* (Ⓦ www.guiadelociobcn.es). The newly-launched *Time Out Barcelona* magazine (Ⓦ www.timeout.cat) is currently only available in Catalan, but is easy to follow. These preview cinema, theatre, music and nightlife for the week, together with extensive sections on bars, restaurants and the city's thriving gay scene. The most comprehensive English-language guides are *Barcelona Metropolitan Magazine* (Ⓦ www.barcelona-metropolitan.com) and *Barcelona Connect* (Ⓦ www.barcelonaconnect.com), both free in pubs, bars, tourist offices and language centres. For online listings in English try *Lecool* magazine (Ⓦ www.lecool.com) and the city council's excellent website (Ⓦ www.bcn.es). The local paper, *La Vanguardia* (Ⓦ www.lavanguardia.es) also has an arts and entertainments page. The leaflet *Informatíu Musical*, available free from tourist offices, record shops and concert venues, is an excellent source of concert and recital information. There is also a cultural information desk at **Palau de la Virreina** (ⓐ La Rambla 99 ❶ 933 017 775).

Tickets are best purchased from the relevant box office at each venue. Alternatively, you can book by phone or via the internet, or purchase from **Servi-Caixa** (☎ 902 332 211 Ⓦ www.serviticket.com) and **Tel-Entrada** (☎ 902 101 212 Ⓦ www.telentrada.com) – operated by two of the city's largest savings banks, La Caixa and Caixa Catalunya. Servi-Caixa has special machines next to La Caixa's ATMs, which print out the tickets; Tel-Entrada is operated out of larger branches of Caixa Catalunya, and at a dedicated desk in the Plaça de Catalunya tourist office.

⬥ *Street sculpture* – Barcelona Head *by Roy Lichtenstein*

Sport & relaxation

SPECTATOR SPORTS

Barcelonans are football crazy and no visit to the city is complete for sports fans without a visit to Camp Nou, home to **FC Barcelona** (ⓦ www.fcbarcelona.com) and one of the great shrines of world football. Other celebrated city teams include the **Barcelona Dragons** (ⓦ www.fcbarcelonaweb.com/dragons), who play in the World League of American Football on Sundays from April to June at the Estadi Olímpic; **DKV Joventut** (ⓦ www.penya.com) and **FC Winterthur Barcelona** (ⓦ www.fcbarcelona.com) are the top basketball teams,

🔺 *Windsurfing on Barceloneta beach*

which play league games on Sunday evenings and European and Spanish Cup matches midweek from September to early June at the Pabellón Olímpico (Olympic Pavilion) in Badalona and the Palau Blaugrana respectively; and **FC Barcelona Pista de Gel** (ⓦ www.fcbarcelona.com), the city's ice hockey team, which plays at the ice rink of the **Camp Nou** complex (ⓔ Av. Joan XXII ❶ 934 963 630 ⓦ www.fcbarcelona.com).

Bullfighting is not popular in Barcelona although the city still has two bullrings: Les Arenes in the Plaça d'Espanya and El Monumental on Carrer Marina. Les Arenes was left derelict for many years but is now being converted into a shopping and leisure centre. Monumental is still in business but the fights, catering to tourists and the local population of Andalucían immigrants, are of a notoriously low standard.

Tickets for major sporting events are available from venues or online at ⓦ www.serviticket.com.

PARTICIPATION SPORTS

The **Centre Municipal de Tennis Vall d'Hebron** (ⓔ Passeig de la Vall D'Hebron 178–196 ❶ 934 276 500) has clay courts open to the public, while **DiR Campus** (ⓔ Av. del Doctor Marañón 17 ❶ 933 016 209 ⓦ www.dir.es) is a general fitness centre that also offers squash courts, racket-ball and basketball.

Several clubs offer weekend sailing and windsurfing courses. Contact **Base Nàutica de la Mar Bella** (ⓔ Av. Litoral ❶ 932 210 432 ⓦ www.basenautica.org). **Piscines Bernat Picornell** (ⓔ Av. de l'Estadi 30–40 ❶ 934 234 041 ⓦ www.picornell.cat) and the seafront **Club de Natació Atlètic Barceloneta** (ⓔ Pl. del Mar ❶ 932 210 010 ⓦ www.cnab.org) are two of several swimming pools open to the public.

Contact the **sports information service** (ⓔ Av. de l'Estadi 30–40 ❶ 934 023 000) for details of city-run sports centres and facilities.

Accommodation

Barcelona offers a wide range of accommodation options, from cool, contemporary boutique and deluxe belle époque palace, to simple B&Bs and hostels. Luxury hotels are generally extremely expensive; quality budget accommodation can be difficult to find even during winter months.

Many affordable hotels are located in the atmospheric Barri Gòtic. Those on or near La Rambla may be noisy at night. The Eixample offers a wider selection, especially in the mid-range price bracket, but these often sacrifice character for functionality. There are no campsites in the city but there are plenty of centrally located youth hostels for budget travellers. Apartment hotels are a good bet for extended stays, especially if you're travelling as a family.

Early booking is essential and breakfasts are usually charged on top. All hotel bills are subject to 7 per cent VAT. There is usually a charge for secure hotel car parking. It is virtually impossible to find a hotel off the street so, if you haven't booked in advance, try the hotel-finding agency **Ultramar Express** (ⓘ 934 914 463 ⓛ 08.00–22.00) in Sants railway station, or the main tourist office in Plaça de Catalunya (see page 152).

HOTELS

Banys Orientals £ The ultimate in urban chic, surprisingly affordable for the heart of fashionable El Born. ⓐ C/ Argenteria 37 (La Barceloneta, El Born & La Ribera) ⓘ 932 688 460 ⓦ www.hotelbanysorientals.com
Ⓜ Metro: Jaume I

El Jardí £ A popular small hotel on one of the Barri Gòtic's most atmospheric squares. Book well in advance for a room with a view.
ⓐ Pl. Sant Josep Oriol 1 (La Rambla & Barri Gòtic) ⓘ 933 015 900
ⓦ www.hoteljardi-barcelona.com Ⓜ Metro: Liceu

PRICE CATEGORIES

The ratings below (unrelated to the official star system) indicate the approximate cost of a room for two people for one night (excluding VAT and breakfast):

£ up to €100   ££ €100–200   £££ over €200

Market Hotel £ Right by the Sant Antoni market, this sleek monochrome hotel is high on design but low on price and comes with a great restaurant. ⓐ Passatge Sant Antoni Abat 10, corner Comte Borrell 68 (L'Eixample & Gràcia) ⓣ 933 251 205 ⓦ www.markethotel.com.es ⓝ Metro: Sant Antoni

Casa Camper ££ A concept boutique hotel from the Camper footwear company with starkly modern décor and plenty of treats such as organic breakfasts, hammocks and bikes for rent. ⓐ C/ Elisabets 11 (La Rambla & Barri Gòtic) ⓣ 933 422 680 ⓦ www.casacamper.com ⓝ Metro: Catalunya

Colón ££ Cosy old-fashioned hotel opposite the cathedral – an excellent choice for families. ⓐ Av. de la Catedral 7 (La Rambla & Barri Gòtic) ⓣ 933 011 404 ⓦ www.hotelcolon.es ⓝ Metro: Jaume I or Urquinaona

Condes de Barcelona ££ Elegant hotel combining *Modernista* architecture with avant-garde décor. ⓐ Passeig de Gràcia 73-75 (L'Eixample & Gràcia) ⓣ 934 450 000 ⓦ www.condesdebarcelona.com ⓝ Metro: Diagonal

Hotel 54 ££ Modern hotel by the beach with unbeatable views of the city, a roof lounge terrace and hip décor in shades of understated grey. ⓐ Passeig Joan de Borbé 54 (La Barceloneta, El Born & La Ribera) ⓣ 932 250 054 ⓦ www.hotel54barceloneta.com ⓝ Metro: Barceloneta

Neri ££ An intimate boutique hotel with state-of-the-art amenities within a characterful 18th-century palace in the Barri Gòtic. ⓐ C/ Sant Sever 5 (La Rambla & Barri Gòtic) ⓣ 933 040 655 ⓦ www.hotelneri.com ⓝ Metro: Jaume I or Liceu

Arts £££ Fashionable hotel beside the sea in one of Spain's tallest buildings, with high-tech facilities and spa. ⓐ C/ de la Marina 19–21 (La Barceloneta, El Born & La Ribera) ⓣ 932 211 000 ⓦ www.hotelartsbarcelona.com ⓝ Metro: Ciutadella Vila Olímpica

La Florida £££ The ultimate romantic getaway – a 5-star historic hotel with post-modern interiors on Tibidabo, with sensational spa, pool and gardens overlooking the city. It is a half-hour drive from the city centre, but a shuttle bus is available for guests. ⓐ Carretera Vallvidrera al Tibidabo 83–93 (Pedralbes, Tibidabo & Les Corts) ⓣ 932 593 000 ⓦ www.hotellaflorida.com

H1898 £££ Very smart 4-star hotel in a majestic 19th-century building bang on the Rambla, with a spa, pools and gym. ⓐ La Rambla 109 (La Rambla & Barri Gòtic) ⓣ 935 529 552 ⓦ www.hotel1898.com ⓝ Metro: Catalunya

Omm £££ Cutting-edge boutique hotel with minimalist interiors, relaxation centre, nightclub, rooftop pool and celebrated restaurant. ⓐ C/ Rosselló 265 (L'Eixample & Gràcia) ⓣ 934 454 000 ⓦ www.hotelomm.es ⓝ Metro: Diagonal

GUESTHOUSES

Hostal Gat Raval £ A funky budget *hostal* in the heart of the Raval, with sparkling clean communal bathrooms, views of the MACBA and bright, sunny rooms. ⓐ C/ Joaquín Costa 44, 2nd floor (Montjuïc & El Raval) ⓣ 934 816 670 ⓦ www.gatrooms.es ⓝ Metro: Universitat

Sagrada Família £ A tiny B&B for those seeking home comforts. ⓐ C/ Nápols 266 (L'Eixample & Gràcia) ⓣ 651 891 413 ⓦ www.sagradafamilia-bedandbreakfast.com ⓝ Metro: Sagrada Família

YOUTH HOSTELS

Centric Point £ Modern youth hostel with broadband, bar, satellite TV and breakfast included. ⓐ Passeig de Gràcia 33 (L'Eixample & Gràcia) ⓣ 932 156 538 ⓦ www.centricpointhostel.com ⓝ Metro: Passeig de Gràcia

🔺 *The striking Arts hotel enjoys a wonderful beachside location*

THE BEST OF BARCELONA

There's plenty in Barcelona to fill even a long city break but if
you have only a few days to spare then here's our list of sights
and experiences you should really try not to miss.

TOP 10 ATTRACTIONS

- **La Sagrada Família** This eccentric temple is an architectural
  marvel, the symbol of the city and Gaudí's most celebrated
  creation (see page 96)

- **Museu Picasso** A comprehensive collection of early artworks
  by Pablo Picasso, from childhood sketches to Cubism, housed
  in five medieval palaces (see page 80)

- **Museu Nacional d'Art de Catalunya (MNAC)** One thousand
  years of Catalan art under one roof – don't miss the decorative
  arts and photography displays (see page 114)

- **Manzana de la Discordia** Just one block holds three *Modernista*
  masterpieces: Gaudí's *Casa Batlló*, Puig i Cadafalch's *Casa
  Ametller* and Domènech i Montaner's *Casa Lleó Morera*
  (see page 92)

- **Park Güell** Antoni Gaudí's flamboyant hilltop park is an extraordinary piece of landscape design, great for family picnics and far-reaching views (see page 94)

- **Fundació Joan Miró** A dazzling gallery devoted to one of Barcelona's finest artists up on Montjuïc hill (see page 111)

- **La Rambla** The most famous boulevard in Spain and the hub of city life for locals and visitors alike (see page 63)

- **El Born and Santa Maria del Mar** The city's 'seaside church' is striking in its simplicity. You'll find it in the trendy El Born area of the city (see pages 75 & 79)

- **Palau de la Música Catalana** One of the city's greatest *Modernista* masterpieces, an internationallly acclaimed concert hall and a UNESCO World Heritage Site (see page 80)

- **Camp Nou** Home of FC Barcelona. If you can't get a ticket for a match, at least visit the museum and take a tour of the stadium (see page 125)

◗ *Detail of the old ticket offices at the Palau de la Música*

Suggested itineraries

HALF-DAY: BARCELONA IN A HURRY

If you have only a few hours, start your visit promenading along the city's most famous boulevard, La Rambla. Then explore the dark atmospheric streets and enchanting squares of the Barri Gòtic. Art lovers should also visit the remarkable collections of Museu Picasso in the neighbouring La Ribera district.

1 DAY: TIME TO SEE A LITTLE MORE

Having completed the half-day itinerary, you are now at the heart of the fashionable La Ribera district with its myriad hip fashion

● La Rambla, Spain's most famous boulevard

boutiques, galleries and design shops, so add some shopping to your day. Alternatively, visit the beautiful church of Santa Maria del Mar or take in a museum. The Museu d'Història de Catalunya is especially interesting. For dinner, head back to the trendy bars and bistros of La Ribera or enjoy more traditional dishes and some of the city's finest seafood in the Barceloneta district.

2–3 DAYS: TIME TO SEE MUCH MORE

These extra days provide plenty of time to explore the city's museums and spectacular *Modernista* architecture. The Eixample district contains many of the most famous buildings. Shopaholics will also enjoy Passeig de Gràcia – the Champs-Élysées of Barcelona – for its exclusive shops and designer boutiques. There are also some excellent tapas bars here for a light lunch, before heading off to admire Gaudí's most celebrated sights – La Sagrada Família and Park Güell.

Or visit Montjuïc hill and spend the day marvelling at such major museums as the Museu Nacional d'Art de Catalunya (MNAC) and the Fundació Joan Miró. Return to the old town for dinner in the Barri Gòtic. You may also have time to explore the rejuvenated waterfront, including Port Vell with its impressive Maremàgnum shopping complex and the ancient royal shipyards of the Museu Marítim.

LONGER: ENJOYING BARCELONA TO THE FULL

A longer stay enables you to soak up the café culture of the old town, to top up your tan on the beaches and to visit some of the outlying districts of town, including Pedralbes with its monastery and museums, and Mont Tibidabo in the Collserola hills. For out of town trips, see page 130.

Something for nothing

Barcelona is an excellent city for budget travellers, with plenty of free sights and attractions. For a taste of Barcelona's history, stroll the narrow maze of alleyways of the medieval Barri Gòtic district; explore the 'open-air museum' district of L'Eixample to marvel at the *Modernista* architecture of the early 20th century; and visit Montjuïc hill to admire the high-tech sporting facilities of the 1992 Olympics. Some museums offer free entry at certain times: the Museu Picasso is free every Sunday from 15.00 (and all day on the first Sunday of the month); Museu Frederic Marès offers free admission from 15.00 every Wednesday and Sunday; and the Museu d'Història de Catalunya is free on the first Sunday of the month. In many ways, the entire city resembles a giant outdoor gallery, with over 400 open-air monuments and sculptures to enjoy.

Shopping fanatics on a budget can enjoy some of the world's finest window-shopping, especially on Passeig de Gràcia, the Diagonal and in La Ribera and El Born. There are also several worthwhile markets to browse, including an antiques market in Plaça del Pi on Thursdays; the weekend art market in Plaça Sant Josep Oriol; the Sunday coin and stamp market in Plaça Reial; the huge flea market of Els Encants at Sant Antoni; and the sensational food market of La Boqueria from Monday to Saturday.

Alternatively, escape the bustle of downtown Barcelona and walk in the Collserola hills or head for the city's beautiful parks. Relax in tranquil Parc de la Ciutadella or admire the sweeping city vistas and unusual sculptures of Gaudí's Park Güell. Many parks contain playgrounds and attractions for children, including Parc de l'Espanya Industrial with its giant dragon slide and a small boating lake, and Parc del Laberint with a fun topiary maze. The city squares are also great places to sit and watch the world go by: feed the pigeons in Plaça de Catalunya; listen to the buskers in Plaça de Sant Josep Oriol; and watch the *sardana* dancers perform in Plaça de la Seu on Saturday at noon and 18.00 or in Plaça Sant Jaume on Sunday at noon. It's also fun to people-watch on La Rambla, and enjoy the lively street entertainment every few paces, ranging from buskers and card sharps to human statues. And on lazy summer days, where better to while away the hours than on Barcelona's fine, sandy beaches?

⬤ *Take a siesta in Park Güell*

When it rains

It rarely rains in Barcelona. On average the city has 300 days of sunshine each year and the tendency is for brief showers rather than day-long downpours. It is more likely that you will want to spend time indoors to get out of the heat than the rain. However,

● *Escape the elements in the Museu Tauri, the bullfighting museum*

come rain or shine, there are plenty of indoor activities to keep you amused.

There are over 50 museums and galleries catering for all ages and interests, from highbrow modern art to football. Immerse yourself in history at the Museu d'Història de la Ciutat or the Museu Marítim; visit one of numerous art galleries, including Museu Picasso, Fundació Joan Miró, the Museu Nacional d'Art de Catalunya and the Museu d'Art Contemporani de Barcelona; or seek refuge from the elements in the Catedral, the Basílica de Santa Maria del Mar or the Monestir de Pedralbes. Children especially enjoy the underwater world at L'Aquàrium; the state-of-the-art IMAX cinema at Port Vell; and Cosmocaixa, the new hands-on science museum and planetarium on the lower slopes of Tibidabo.

Barcelona's shopping ranks among the best in the world, and there are several large department stores and shopping centres to occupy any keen shopper for hours, including El Corte Inglés, Spain's main department store, with branches throughout the city; Maremàgnum at Port Vell; and a number of exclusive shopping malls off Passeig de Gràcia and La Rambla de Catalunya.

If that sounds too energetic, relax at a beauty spa. The Six Senses Spa at Hotel Arts and the ZenZone Spa at the Gran Hotel La Florida offer the ultimate in pampering. Or join locals in one of the numerous bars and cafés. Take your pick of refreshment in spacious trendy 'design-bars'; *xampanyerias* (champagne bars); cosy old-fashioned bodegas, serving wine from the barrel; traditional tapas bars; and *cervecerías* (beer bars). Or simply master the Barcelonan art of coffee drinking in one of the characterful locals' cafés: try *cafè amb llet* (a large milky coffee) for breakfast; a *tallat* (a small coffee with a dash of milk) or a *cafè* (espresso) at midday; and a *cigaló* (an espresso with a shot of brandy unless you specify another liqueur) after dinner.

On arrival

ARRIVING

By air

Barcelona's airport, **El Prat de Llobregat** (☎ 932 983 838 ⓦ www.aena.es) is situated 12 km (8 miles) southwest of Barcelona. The most convenient way to reach the city centre from the airport is by taxi. This takes around 20–30 minutes but it is the most expensive option. There is also a regular Aerobús bus service every 6-15 minutes (🕓 06.00–01.00) from the airport to Plaça de Catalunya, via Plaça d'Espanya, Gran Via de les Corts Catalanes and Plaça de la Universitat. Tickets are available from the driver and the journey takes about 30-40 minutes. The return ticket is valid for a week.

At rush hour, the regular rail service is generally a quicker option. Note that due to ongoing building work for the AVE high speed train, the only train running from the airport is the C2 to Barcelona–Sants and Passeig de Gràcia stations, both of which connect with the metro. Journey time is 20 minutes and trains leave at 8 and 38 minutes past the hour from 06.08 to 23.38.

By rail

The city's main railway station, **Barcelona–Sants** (❷ Pl. dels Països Catalans ❶ 934 956 215), is the main arrival point from both national and international destinations, and also connects with the metro network. Facilities include tourist information, hotel information,

❍ *A quiet moment at Barcelona airport*

Barcelona

a bank, restaurants, shops, first-aid and left-luggage lockers. Other major railway stations in the city include **Estació de França** (🚇 Av. Marqués de l'Argentera), near Barceloneta metro station, and Estació Passeig de Gràcia, near Plaça de Catalunya.

By road

Eurolines (📞 902 405 040 🌐 www.eurolines.es) provide coach links to most major Spanish cities as well as the rest of Europe. Coaches stop at both **Barcelona Nord** (🚌 C/ d'Alí Bei 80 🌐 www.barcelonanord.com) and **Estació Autobuses de Sants** (🚌 C/ Viriato 📞 934 904 000) beside the main Sants railway station. A variety of coach companies have offices based at Barcelona Nord.

   If you are driving, the A7 motorway is the main route to Barcelona from France, while the A2 joins Zaragoza to the west, with connections

---

IF YOU GET LOST, TRY SOME CASTILLIAN SPANISH

Excuse me, do you speak English?
Perdone, ¿habla inglés?
Perdoneh, ¿ahbla eengless?

Excuse me, is this the right way to the old town/the city centre/ the tourist office/the station/the bus station?
Perdone, ¿por aquí se va al casco antiguo/al centro de la ciudad/ a la oficina de turismo/la estación de trenes/estación de autobuses?
Perdoneh, ¿porr akee seh bah ah el kasko antigwo/al thentroe de la theeoodath/a la offeetheena deh toorismoe/la estatheeon de trenes/estatheeon dey awtoebooses?

---

from Madrid. The Barcelona ring road makes it easy to approach the city centre from all directions but, once in the centre, driving can be quite daunting with fast multi-lane avenues and complicated one-way systems. Parking can also be difficult and car parks are expensive. Your best bet is to find a space marked in blue with a *Zona Blava* (Blue Zone) sign and to purchase a ticket from a nearby parking meter. Parking costs around €2–4 per hour.

FINDING YOUR FEET

Barcelona appears to be a bustling Mediterranean city but the pace of life here is surprisingly relaxed. As with most major cities, there are incidents of petty crime, so it is advisable to take common sense precautions (see page 145).

ORIENTATION

Barcelona is easy to navigate as it's divided into districts, each with distinctive characteristics, and the public transport system is efficient. You may get lost in the labyrinth of narrow streets and dark alleys of the Barri Gòtic and La Ribera, but that is half the fun. Arm yourself with a good map and make sure you know where the boundary thoroughfare of Via Laietana is located! L'Eixample can be a little confusing as it's built on a grid system with extremely long avenues and identical-looking blocks of buildings. Wherever you are in the city, there are certain unmissable landmarks, though, such as the sea, Montjuïc hill and Mont Tibidabo.

GETTING AROUND

The metro network, operated by **TMB** (Ⓦ www.tmb.cat) is the most efficient means of transport in the city. It is easy to use, with seven lines, each identified by a number and a colour, and the

direction is indicated by the end-station of each line. The metro runs 05.00–00.00 Sunday to Thursday, 05.00–02.00 Friday, and 24 hours on Saturdays and public holidays. TMB also operate several tram lines. The uptown lines cover the areas of Les Corts and Pedralbes, while the downtown lines cover the Vila Olímpica, Glòries and the Fòrum.

For the suburbs and surrounding areas there are regional rail lines run by the **Ferrocarrils de la Generalitat de Catalunya** (FGC ⓦ www.fgc.es) and RENFE. The FGC line is fully integrated into the metro system and runs 05.45–00.00 Sunday to Thursday and 05.50–02.15 on Fridays and Saturdays, although times vary for different lines. The main station for regional trains is Catalunya, located under Plaça de Catalunya at the top of La Rambla. Buy tickets from ticket offices and automatic vending machines at each station. Remember to validate your ticket in a machine on the platform before boarding.

There is also an extensive bus network, operated by TMB (ⓒ 06.30–22.00), with most services passing through Plaça de Catalunya, Plaça Urquinaona or Plaça de la Universitat. Purchase your tickets from the driver and validate them in the machines on the buses. The city's 16 night-bus routes, which run approximately every half-hour from 23.00–04.00, require separate tickets.

If you intend to use the bus and metro frequently, consider one of the special multi-ride tickets available from metro ticket offices, automatic vending machines and FGC railway stations. These include the T-10 for 10 journeys; a T-día one-day pass and also special tourist passes, valid for two, three, four and five days, which cover all transport in the city, including the journey to and from the airport. The Barcelona Card offers unlimited use of public transport for up to five days and discounts on the Aerobús and cable cars along with reduced entry to various museums and attractions.

The **Bus Turístic** (ⓣ 932 853 832 ⓦ www.tmb.cat) is an easy way to get around, with 42 hop-on, hop-off stops. The two main routes, North and South, start from Plaça de Catalunya and last about two hours if you don't get off. The buses run every 6–20 minutes depending on the season, from 09.00–19.00 or until 20.00 in the summer months. A third route covers the Fòrum area and runs 09.30–19.00, April to September only. A new night route has been introduced to show off Barcelona's illuminated buildings, leaving Plaça de Catalunya at 21.10 from May to September. Standard tickets are valid for two days and cost €20 for adults and €12 for children aged 4–12.

Look out also for the TombBús – a special shopping service that runs every 7 minutes on weekdays (🕐 07.30–21.58) and every 15 minutes on Saturdays (🕐 09.30–21.45) between Plaça de Catalunya and Plaça Pius XII.

🔽 Street art on Montjuïc hill

To get to Montjuïc, you can choose between the funicular railway from Avinguda Paral.lel to Avinguda Miramar (🕐 09.00–20.00, or 22.00 in summer) and a *telefèric* (cable car) to Montjuïc castle (🕐 11.00–19.15). Another cable car, the Transbordador Aeri, runs from La Barceloneta to Miramar (🕐 11.00–20.00 summer; 10.45–19.00 winter). Among Barcelona's other novel transport options are the Golondrinas pleasure boat tours (see page 77), the ancient Tramvia Blau (Blue Tram, see page 124), and the Funicular de Tibidabo (see page 124).

Black-and-yellow taxis can be hailed in the street or booked in advance, but they are an expensive option. Those that are free have a green light on the roof and a sign saying *lliure/libre* in the front window. Reliable companies include **Radio Taxi** (🕿 933 033 033) and **Servitaxi** (🕿 933 300 300). Alternatively, hire a bicycle from **Un Coxte Menys** (🖂 C/ Esparteria 3 🕿 932 682 105 🌐 www.bicicletabarcelona.com) at around €5 an hour or €15 a day.

Lastly, an eco-friendly way to get around the city is the **Trixi rickshaws** (🕿 93 310 1379 🌐 www.trixi.com 🕐 12.00–20.00 Apr–Sept). These can be booked by phone or hailed on the street, usually from around the Catedral or near the beach.

CAR HIRE

It's only worthwhile hiring a car if you're planning to explore Catalonia. There are several car rental companies at the airport, although pre-booking with your airline's affiliates should secure you reduced rates.

Avis 🖂 Terminals B & C 🕿 932 983 601 🌐 www.avis.es
Europcar 🖂 Terminals B & C 🕿 932 983 300 🌐 www.europcar.es
Hertz 🖂 Terminals B & C 🕿 932 983 637 🌐 www.hertz.es
National Atesa 🖂 Terminals B & C 🕿 932 983 433 🌐 www.atesa.es

▶ *La Barceloneta waterfront*

THE CITY OF
Barcelona

La Rambla & Barri Gòtic

Sooner or later, all visitors to Barcelona find themselves strolling with locals on La Rambla, Spain's most famous and well-trodden boulevard, abuzz with flower stalls, artists and street entertainers. It leads through the heart of the old city down to the port. Just off La Rambla, the Barri Gòtic (Gothic Quarter) is Barcelona's oldest district, brimming with atmospheric streets, alleyways and hidden squares, and flanked by countless buildings of historical interest. The Barri Gòtic is something of a misnomer as the district combines its splendid Gothic architecture with Roman, Romanesque and Renaissance elements, making it a fascinating area to explore.

SIGHTS & ATTRACTIONS

Catedral (Cathedral)

Barcelona's mighty Gothic cathedral was constructed on the remains of a palaeo-Christian basilica and a Romanesque church. Dedicated to St Eulàlia, who was martyred by the Romans in the fourth century for her Christian beliefs, it is considered one of the finest examples of Catalan Gothic architecture.

The majestic interior is a harmonious fusion of medieval and Renaissance style, and the Chapel of Christ of Lepanto is its finest example of Gothic architecture. Eulàlia herself lies in the subterranean alabaster crypt below the altar. Don't miss the tranquil 14th-century cloister, with its shaded gardens, pond and even a small gaggle of 13 white Roman geese, representing Eulàlia's age and the 13 grisly punishments meted out to her by the Roman emperor.

Entrance is free during the hours given below, but purchasing a combined ticket will allow you to enter 13.00–17.00 Mon–Sat and

14.00–16.45 Sun, when the cathedral is officially closed to non-paying visitors. A combined ticket also allows you to take photographs, enter the choir and some of the private side chapels, and use the lift to the roof for the view. ⓐ Pl. de la Seu ❶ 933 151 554 ⓦ www.catedralbcn.org ⓒ Church: 08.00–12.45, 17.15–19.00 Mon–Fri (18.00 Sat & Sun); museum: 10.00–12.30, 17.15–19.00; cloister: 09.00–12.30, 17.00–19.00 Ⓝ Metro: Liceu or Jaume I

Monument a Colom

This monumental column at the seaward end of Las Ramblas is crowned by a statue of Christopher Columbus, pointing to the horizon with an outstretched arm. It commemorates the great navigator's return to Barcelona from his first voyage to the Americas in 1492. It was erected outside the naval headquarters of Catalonia during the 1888 Universal Exhibition and from the top it affords spectacular views of the seafront. ⓐ Pl. Portal de la Pau ❶ 933 025 224 ⓒ 09.00–20.30 June–Sept; 09.00–20.00 Oct–May Ⓝ Metro: Drassanes

Plaça del Rei

The delightful 'King's Square' was once a busy medieval marketplace. Today it is a fascinating ensemble of architectural styles. One side is occupied by the Palau Reial Major (Great Royal Palace), the former residence of the Counts of Barcelona, constructed in the 11th century. It was on the steps leading up to the palace that King Ferdinand and Queen Isabella are believed to have received Columbus on his return from the Americas in 1492. On the north side of the square, the Gothic Capella de Santa Àgata (Chapel of St Agatha) was constructed on the old Roman wall. Opposite, the Palau del Lloctinent (Palace of the Viceroy) was built in 1549 for the Catalan representative of the king.

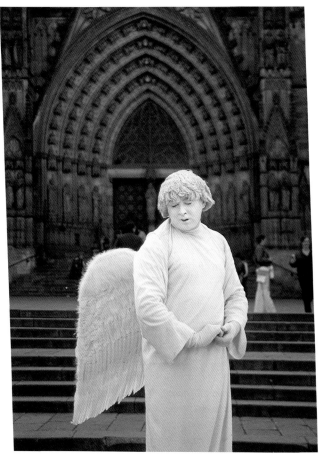

◯ *Human statue outside the Catedral*

The five-storey Mirador de Rei Martí (Tower of King Martí) stands tall above the square but is not open to the public. The Museu d'Història de la Ciutat (City History Museum, see page 66) is also in the square.
ⓐ Pl. del Rei Ⓜ Metro: Jaume I

Plaça Reial

This charming porticoed square, flanked by bars and restaurants and adorned by palm trees and an ornamental fountain, was constructed in 1848. Some of the façades are decorated with sculpted terracotta reliefs of celebrated navigators and the two tree-like central lampposts were Gaudí's first commission in Barcelona. On Sunday mornings there is a coin and stamp market here. Be warned that at night it can get a little scuzzy and there is a high presence of pickpockets.
ⓐ Pl. Reial Ⓜ Metro: Liceu

Plaça de Sant Jaume

This square is situated on the site of the former forum and marketplace of Roman *Barcino*. Today it represents the city's political hub. On its south side stands the impressive Catalan Gothic Ajuntament (Town Hall), seat of the city's government. Across the square, the Renaissance Palau de la Generalitat (Government Palace) is home to the government of Catalonia.
ⓐ Pl. de Sant Jaume Ⓜ Metro: Jaume I

Plaça de la Seu (Cathedral Square)

Also known as Plaça de la Catedral, this spacious square is a popular meeting point and also draws a number of buskers and street entertainers. On Sundays, locals gather at 12.00 and 18.00 to perform the *sardana*, a curiously sedate Catalan folk dance, before the cathedral's ornate and imposing façade, which appears to be constantly undergoing renovation works. Between the east side of the cathedral and Via Laietana lie the remnants of the ancient Roman walls. ❷ Pl. de la Seu Ⓜ Metro: Liceu or Jaume I

La Rambla

This magnificent 18th-century tree-lined promenade – with its cafés, buskers, newsstands, street artists and bustling crowds of locals and tourists – is where the city's heart beats loudest. La Rambla is among the Mediterranean's most celebrated boulevards, and the pride of Barcelona, although even its most ardent fans admit that it has become a little down-at-heel of late. Part of the council's recent clean-up campaign has included the renovation of the Miró floor mosaic

⬥ *Charming Plaça Reial, constructed in 1848*

WHAT'S IN A NAME?
The name 'Rambla' is derived from *ramla* (Arabic for 'sand'),
named after the sandy stream bed here that ran parallel with
the medieval city walls, carrying rainwater down to the sea.
Dry during summer months, this route soon became the
main link to the harbour. In the 14th century, it was eventually
paved. Such is its significance today that the Barcelonans have
coined two new words – *ramblejar*, to walk down the Rambla
and *ramblista*, someone who loves to *ramblejar*.

outside the Liceu opera house, a greater police presence to deter the
pickpockets and quality controls on the human statues and artists.
La Rambla is also known as Les Rambles/Las Ramblas as it is divided
into five sections, each with its own characteristics. Descending
from Plaça de Catalunya they are: Rambla de Canaletes, named after
the famous little iron fountain – one sip allegedly ensures your return
to the city; Rambla dels Estudis, colloquially known as Rambla dels
Ocells because of the bird stalls; Rambla de Sant Josep, also called
Rambla de les Flors because of the flower stalls and best known for
the Boqueria market and Liceu opera house; Rambla dels Caputxins;
and Rambla Santa Mònica, which is filled with caricature artists.
ⓐ La Rambla ⓜ Metro: Catalunya, Liceu or Drassanes

Temple Romà d'Agusti
Housed in the headquarters of the Catalan hiking club lies one of the
great secrets of Roman Barcelona, virtually unvisited by the hordes of
nearby tourists: four jaw-dropping fluted Corinthian columns dating
from the first century BC. Historians agree that they once formed the

back corner of the Temple of Augustus and stood at the very heart of the Forum of Roman *Barcino*. Marking the central spot is an old millstone just by the entrance of the building. ➌ C/ Paradís 10 ➊ 933 151 111 ⏰ 11.00–18.00 Mon–Fri, 11.00–15.00 Sat & Sun Ⓜ Metro: Jaume I

CULTURE

Gran Teatre del Liceu

For over 150 years, the Liceu has been Spain's foremost opera house, hosting world-class performers from Montserrat Caballé to José Carreras ever since its inauguration in 1847. However, it has an extremely chequered history: it was tragically burned down in 1861, and rebuilt only to be bombed in 1893. It was restored to its former glory, then went up in flames again in 1994. Once more it rose from the ashes in 1999, but this time with improved acoustics, a larger stage and state-of-the-art machinery. Guided tours of the interior provide a unique insight into the workings of the theatre. ➌ La Rambla 51–59 ➊ 934 859 900 Ⓦ www.liceubarcelona.com ⏰ Full tour: 10.00 (1 hr 10 mins); express tours: 11.30, 12.00, 13.00 (20 mins) Ⓜ Metro: Liceu

Museu Frederic Marès (Frederic Marès Museum)

This eccentric museum, at the heart of the Gothic Quarter, was founded and donated to the city by sculptor and private collector of all manner of curios, Frederic Marès i Deulovol (1893–1991). It comprises two sections: the sculpture collection, with artefacts from pre-Roman times through to the 20th century; and the 'Sentimental Museum', portraying daily life from the 15th to the 20th centuries through an extraordinary array of curios and household objects. Entrance to the museum is via a beautiful medieval courtyard garden, once part of the Royal Palace of the Kings and Queens of Catalonia and Aragon.

Pl. Sant Iu 5–6 933 105 800 www.museumares.bcn.cat
10.00–19.00 Tues–Sat, 10.00–15.00 Sun Metro: Jaume I.
Admission charge

Museu d'Història de la Ciutat (City History Museum)

This fascinating museum recounts the city's evolution through 2,000 years of history, in a series of locations around the Plaça del Rei (see page 60). Start at the impressive underground walkways beneath the square, which reveal the ancient foundations of the Roman settlement of Barcino.

The main section of the museum is housed in a medieval mansion, and vividly traces the story of Barcelona from a simple Roman trading post to a wealthy 18th-century metropolis. The museum ticket also includes entry to the Saló del Tinell, which is the spacious barrel-vaulted banqueting hall of the Palau Reial Major, and to the Capella de Santa Àgata, which is the royal chapel. Pl. del Rei, C/ del Veguer 2 933 151 111 www.museuhistoria.bcn.cat 10.00–20.00 Tues–Sun, Apr–Sept; 10.00–14.00, 16.00–19.00 Tues–Sun, Oct–Mar Metro: Jaume I. Admission charge.

RETAIL THERAPY

There are plenty of shops to choose from here, from the fashion boutiques of stylish Avinguda Portal de l'Àngel, a busy pedestrian thoroughfare, to the more old-fashioned specialist stores of the Barri Gotìc. Here too, La Boqueria market (see opposite) is the best of over 40 food markets in town, and a must-see, even if you're not hungry.

L'Arca de l'Àvia A treasure trove of antique cottons, linens and silks. C/ Banys Nous 20 933 021 598 www.larcadelavia.com

MERCAT DE LA BOQUERIA

Barcelona's main covered market is a veritable showcase for Catalan gastronomy, from fruit, herbs and vegetables to meat, fish and crustaceans. The cavernous market hall is best entered through an impressive wrought-iron gateway off La Rambla. Inside it's a riot of noise and activity, as market sellers, local shoppers, restaurateurs and tourists all jostle for the best buys of the day. It is an excellent place to stock up for a picnic or simply to soak up the flavours, colours and fragrances.
ⓐ La Rambla 100 ⓣ 933 182 017 ⓦ www.boqueria.info
ⓛ 07.00–20.00 Mon–Sat ⓜ Metro: Liceu ⓘ Some stalls open mornings only

⬤ *La Boqueria, a showcase for Catalan gastronomy*

🕐 17.00–20.00 Mon, 11.00–14.00, 17.00–20.00 Tues–Fri, 11.00–14.00 Sat Ⓜ Metro: Liceu

Art Escudellers Glass and ceramic ware that is largely handmade by Spanish artisans and displayed by region. 📍 C/ Escudellers 23–25 ☎ 934 126 801 🌐 www.escudellers-art.com 🕐 11.00–23.00 Ⓜ Metro: Drassanes

Artur Ramon Anticuario Browse the paintings, furniture and valuable *objets d'art* in Barcelona's best antique store. 📍 C/ de la Palla 25 ☎ 933 025 970 🌐 www.arturamon.com 🕐 10.00–13.30, 17.00–20.00 Mon–Fri, 10.00–13.30 Sat Ⓜ Metro: Liceu or Jaume I

Casa Beethoven Specialist music shop with an impressive stock of scores and sheet music, especially by Spanish and Catalan composers. 📍 La Rambla 97 ☎ 933 014 826 🌐 www.casabeethoven.com 🕐 09.00–14.00, 16.00–20.00 Mon–Fri, 09.00–13.30, 17.00–17.45 Sat Ⓜ Metro: Liceu

Cereria Subirà The city's oldest shop, founded in 1761, sells a staggering variety of candles. 📍 Baixada de la Llibereteria 7 ☎ 933 152 606 🕐 09.00–13.30, 14.00–19.30 Mon–Fri, 09.00–13.30 Sat Ⓜ Metro: Jaume I

La Manual Alpargatera An old-fashioned shop producing all manner of straw-woven items, including handmade traditional *espardenyes* (espadrilles) with esparto soles. 📍 C/ d'Avinyó 7 ☎ 933 010 172 🌐 www.lamanual.net 🕐 09.30–13.30, 16.30–20.00 Mon–Fri, 10.00–13.30, 16.30–20.00 Sat Ⓜ Metro: Jaume I

Sala Parés Barcelona's top gallery, which once held an exhibition by the young Picasso, specialises in 19th- and 20th-century artworks.

ⓐ C/ Petritxol 5 ⓣ 933 187 020 ⓦ www.salapares.com ⓛ 16.00–20.00
Mon, 10.30–14.00, 16.00–20.00 Tues–Fri, 10.30–14.00, 16.30–20.30 Sat
ⓝ Metro: Liceu

TAKING A BREAK

Bar del Pi £ ❶ This pint-sized bar serves delicious coffee and a small
selection of tapas alfresco. ⓐ Pl. de Sant Josep Oriol 1 ⓣ 933 022 123
ⓦ www.bardelpi.com ⓛ 09.00–23.00 Tues–Fri, 09.30–23.00 Sat,
10.00–22.00 Sun ⓝ Metro: Liceu

La Clandestina £ ❷ New age tea house with juices, lassis and
homemade cakes and pastries. Look out for the trapeze acts overhead.
ⓐ Baixada Viladecols, off C/ Hostal d'en Sol behind the Central Post
Office ⓣ 933 190 533 ⓛ 10.00–22.00 Mon–Thur, 10.00–00.00 Fri &
Sat, 11.00–22.00 Sun ⓝ Metro: Jaume I

La Granja £ ❸ A classic milk bar with antique décor (there's even a
section of Roman wall at the back) specialising in gloopy hot chocolate
– try the spicy version with chilli. ⓐ C/ Banys Nous 4 ⓣ 933 026 975
ⓛ 09.00–13.30, 17.00–21.00 Mon–Sat, 17.00–22.00 Sun ⓝ Metro: Liceu

AFTER DARK

RESTAURANTS
Can Culleretes £ ❹ Enjoy robust country-style Catalan cuisine in
an atmospheric, rustic setting in one of the city's oldest restaurants.
Game is a speciality in season. ⓐ C/ d'en Quintana 5 ⓣ 933 176 485
ⓦ www.culleretes.com ⓛ 13.30–16.00, 21.00–23.00 Tues–Sat,
13.30–16.00 Sun ⓝ Metro: Liceu

La Fonda £ ❺ A buzzy designer restaurant serving a good variety of stylish yet affordable Mediterranean dishes. ⓐ C/ Escudellers 10 ❶ 933 017 515 Ⓦ www.lafonda-restaurant.com ❶ 13.00–15.30, 20.30–23.30 Ⓝ Metro: Drassanes ❶ No reservations

Les Quinze Nits £ ❻ One of the Ciutat Vella's most popular restaurants. Ask for a table on the terrace overlooking the square, and tuck into a delicious seafood platter, paella or rabbit stew. Be prepared to queue. ⓐ Pl. Reial 5 ❶ 933 173 075 Ⓦ www.lesquinzenits.com ❶ 13.00–15.30, 20.30–23.30 Ⓝ Metro: Liceu ❶ No reservations

Cafè de l'Acadèmia ££ ❼ With a beautiful little terrace in a quiet church square, this is a wonderful place for a great set lunch or dinner of Catalan cooking with an innovative twist. ⓐ C/ Lleó 1 ❶ 933 198 253 ❶ 13.30–16.30, 20.30–23.30 Mon–Fri Ⓝ Metro: Jaume I

Pitarra ££ ❽ This old-fashioned restaurant, named after the 19th-century Catalan playwright, Frederic 'Pitarra' Soler, who once lived here, is known for its delicious paella. ⓐ C/ d'Avinyó 56 ❶ 933 011 647 Ⓦ www.restaurantpitarra.cat ❶ 13.00–16.00, 20.30–23.00 Mon–Sat Ⓝ Metro: Jaume I

Els Quatre Gats ££ ❾ Local artists and writers popularised this beautiful *Modernista* café in the early 1900s. Even the menu was designed by Picasso. Today the restaurant at the back serves simple Catalan staples. ⓐ C/ de Montsió 3 ❶ 933 024 140 Ⓦ www.4gats.com ❶ 13.00–01.00 Ⓝ Metro: Catalunya

Taxidermista ££ ❿ A lively restaurant in an old taxidermist's studio, offering modern Mediterranean cuisine amid original cast-iron pillars

and marble floors. 🅐 Pl. Reial 8 🅣 934 124 536 🅦 www.xidermista.com
🅛 Restaurant: 13.30–16.00, 19.30–00.00 Tues–Thur & Sun, 13.30–16.00,
19.30–00.30 Fri & Sat; tapas: 13.00–01.00 🅜 Metro: Liceu

Neri Restaurant £££ ⓫ Stone Gothic arches, crushed velvet curtains
and delicate Mediterranean dishes from Jordi Ruiz make for a perfect
romantic dinner. 🅐 C/ Sant Sever 5 🅣 933 040 655 🅦 www.hotelneri.com
🅛 12.00–16.30, 20.30–23.00 🅜 Metro: Jaume I

BARS & CLUBS

Café del Òpera The best café-bar on La Rambla – atmospheric,
intimate and still with its original 19th-century décor. 🅐 La Rambla 74
🅣 933 177 585 🅦 www.cafeoperabcn.com 🅛 08.30–02.30 🅜 Metro: Liceu

Ginger A gem of a bar with hip jazzy sounds, deep yellow leather
armchairs and a great range of cocktails and designer tapas.
🅐 C/ Palma de Sant Just 1 🅣 933 105 309 🅛 19.00–02.30 Tues–Thur,
19.00–03.00 Fri & Sat 🅜 Metro: Jaume I

Jamboree A hugely popular venue for live blues, jazz, soul, funk and
occasional hip-hop until midnight, when it becomes a funky dance
club. The adjoining Tarantos bar develops from flamenco joint to
lively salsa club as the night progresses. 🅐 Pl. Reial 17 🅣 933 191 789
🅦 www.masimas.com/jamboree 🅛 20.00–late; hours vary
depending on event 🅜 Metro: Liceu

Milk This laid-back, baroque-style café-bar serves up great cocktails
and light snacks along with a popular Sunday brunch of smoothies and
pancakes. 🅐 C/ d'en Gignàs 21 🅣 932 680 922 🅦 www.milkbarcelona.com
🅛 18.00–03.00 Mon–Fri, 11.00–03.00 Sat & Sun 🅜 Metro: Jaume I

La Barceloneta, El Born & La Ribera

With so much to see and do in the old town, it is easy to forget that Barcelona is a seaside city, with its fine sandy beaches, marinas and the giant waterfront leisure complexes of the Parc del Fòrum and the Maremàgnum. La Ribera (The Waterfront) was the medieval city's thriving maritime and trading district. In the tenth century, a settlement grew up here along what was then the seashore. Nowadays, it is a smart, in-vogue *barri* (quarter), brimming with trendy boutiques and sophisticated bars and restaurants.

The atmospheric neighbouring district of La Barceloneta was constructed on a triangular wedge of reclaimed land in the mid-18th century. With its narrow streets and ramshackle houses, over the centuries it has retained all the charm of an old Mediterranean fishing village, although it is now in the process of gentrification. It boasts some of the finest seafood restaurants in town.

SIGHTS & ATTRACTIONS

L'Aquàrium de Barcelona (Barcelona Aquarium)

Barcelona's ultra-modern aquarium houses Europe's most important collection of Mediterranean marine life, with over 10,000 exotic sea creatures. The highlight is the 80 m (260 ft) glass tunnel, called the Oceanari, where a moving conveyor belt passes underneath sharks, sting rays, moonfish and other multicoloured species. ⓐ Moll d'Espanya ⓘ 932 217 474 Ⓦ www.aquariumbcn.com Ⓛ 09.30–21.00 Ⓝ Metro: Drassanes or Barceloneta. Admission charge

La Barceloneta

The quaint old district of La Barceloneta (Little Barcelona) was

La Barceloneta, El Born & La Ribera

0 | 500 metres
0 | 500 yards

POI
Metro Stop
Cathedral
Information
Police Station
Airport
Railway Stn
Bus Station
Hospital

traditionally the home of seamen and port workers, and the clock tower on the Moll de la Barceloneta was once a lighthouse. Although the area has been greatly gentrified in recent years, the criss-cross grid of ancient narrow streets still holds children playing football while locals sit and chat, their washing fluttering overhead on the wrought-iron balconies. The heart of the district is the Plaça de la Barceloneta, with the beautiful baroque church of Sant Miquel del Port (Barceloneta's patron saint) and the newly rebuilt municipal market in the enormous central square of Plaça de la Font. Ⓝ Metro: Barceloneta

Beaches
Barcelona's beaches offer bathers and sun-worshippers some of the cleanest city sea-bathing in the Mediterranean, with nearly 5 km (3 miles) of broad, sandy beaches stretching from La Barceloneta northwards. Facilities include lifeguards, public toilets and showers (some accessible for people with disabilities), beach bars known as *xiringuitos*, shops and restaurants. On Platja de Barceloneta there is a new beach centre and small library (with some publications in English) that lends out magazines and newspapers along with beach toys in the summer months. The three beaches nearest the city – Platjes Sant Miquel, Sant Sebastià and Barceloneta – get very crowded on hot days, so it is worth heading further north, off Avinguda del Litoral, to Platjes Nova Icària, Bogatell, Mar Bella (a nudist beach) or Nova Mar Bella, where there are windsurfers and small craft for hire during summer months.

The city has even created a new beach, Llevant, at the northernmost end of the city limits, which is very quiet although it does suffer from an ugly backdrop of high-rise apartment blocks. The most central beaches are fringed by the Passeig Marítim – the palm-lined boardwalk linking La Barceloneta to La Vila Olímpica, the 'twin towers' of the Arts hotel and the Mapfre building, signposted by Frank Gehry's glittering copper *Fish* sculpture – the city's maritime symbol.

🅜 Metro: Barceloneta, Ciutadella Vila Olímpica or Bogatell

El Born (The Born)

The tiny 'Born' district has recently emerged as one of the trendier quarters of town, buzzing by day with funky shops, galleries and

🔺 *Stroll along the quayside in La Barceloneta*

craft workshops, and with fashionable bars and restaurants by night. Its main thoroughfare is the Passeig del Born. The name of this avenue means 'to joust' and for many centuries from the Middle Ages onwards, it was the scene of many city festivals, processions, tournaments, fairs, markets and carnivals. During the Inquisition, heretics were burned here. Today it plays host to a number of popular cafés and restaurants.

One end of the Passeig is dominated by the imposing church of Santa Maria del Mar (see page 79). At the other end, the old Mercat del Born (Born Market) – a glass and wrought-iron structure from the 1870s – is a magnificent example of 19th-century industrial architecture. Until 1977, it housed the city's main wholesale food market. Then, in 2002, building works originally intended to convert the market into a library uncovered some of the most extensive medieval archaeological remains in Europe. Ⓝ Metro: Barceloneta or Jaume I

Fòrum

Built for the six-month symposium known as the 2004 Forum of Cultures, this vast business and leisure complex transformed a large swathe of post-industrial wasteland by the sea. The landmark building is the Edifici Fòrum by Herzog and DeMeuron (who designed London's Tate Modern), a horizontal blue triangle covered in flowing water. The nearby Parc Diagonal Mar was designed by Enric Miralles (who designed the Scottish Parliament Building) and contains a bizarre angular lake and twirling aluminium tubing. Other features include a lido where you can swim out to the Illa Pangea, an island 60 metres (200 ft) from the shore. The large open spaces now provide an excellent venue for music festivals such as Primavera Sound (see page 10). Ⓝ Metro: El Maresme/Fòrum

Las Golondrinas

The best way to see the old harbour and port area is to climb aboard one of the tour boats called *golondrinas* (swallows). Harbour tours depart regularly in summer and once an hour on winter weekends; excursions to the Port Olímpic and the Fòrum operate several times a day during summer. ❷ Pl. Portal de la Pau ❶ 934 423 106 Ⓦ www.lasgolondrinas.com Ⓝ Metro: Drassanes

Parc de la Ciutadella (Citadel Park)

This large leafy park is the green lung of Barcelona. It takes its name from the mighty citadel that dominated the city in the 18th century. In its midst are a boating lake, playgrounds, lawns, promenades, the Parc Zoològic (see below) and a showy fountain – the Font Monumental – which Gaudí contributed to as a student. Notable buildings include the arsenal of the former citadel and the Castell dels Tres Dragons (Three Dragons Castle), a striking *Modernista* building that contains the **Museu de Ciènces Naturals** (Natural History Museum ❶ 933 196 912 Ⓦ www.bcn.es/museuciencies Ⓛ 10.00–18.30 Tues–Sat, 10.00–14.30 Sun Ⓝ Metro: Arc de Triomf. Admission charge). The museum may be transferred to the Fòrum in the future.

Parc Zoològic (Zoo)

Spain's leading zoo, with over 7,500 animals of 400 different species from all over the world, is always a popular outing with children, especially the under-fives who love the petting farm, the mini-train and the splashy shows of the dolphinarium. ❷ Parc de la Ciutadella ❶ 932 256 780 Ⓦ www.zoobarcelona.com Ⓛ 10.00–19.00 June–Sept; 10.00–18.00 Mar–May & Oct; 10.00–17.00 Nov–Feb Ⓝ Metro: Ciutadella Vila Olímpica. Admission charge

Port Vell (Old Port)

No other single Olympic project changed the face of the city as dramatically as the construction of Port Vell. This former industrial area of ships and sprawling warehouses has undergone a massive transformation and is now a popular recreation area, with an aquarium, a cinema complex and Maremàgnum (see page 81), a huge shopping centre with cafés, bars and restaurants. Approach it via the Rambla de Mar, a series of undulating wooden walkways and wavelike metal arches, which stretches out over the sea like a watery extension of La Rambla (see page 58). ⓜ Metro: Drassanes

⬥ *Street sculpture –* Gambrinus *by Xavier Mariscal*

Santa Maria del Mar (Holy Mary of the Sea)

The magnificent Gothic Basilica of Santa Maria del Mar is arguably Barcelona's finest church, striking in its simplicity. It lies at the heart of La Ribera. The original settlement grew up around a tiny tenth-century chapel here called Santa Maria de les Arenes (Holy Mary of the Sands), built on what was then the seashore. During the 14th century, it was transformed into today's imposing 'seaside church' as a show of the city's maritime power. The foundation stone commemorates the Catalan conquest of Sardinia.

The plain façade belies a majestic spacious interior of slim octagonal columns and narrow lofty naves. The church is surprisingly lacking in ornamentation, as most of its treasures were lost during the Spanish Civil War. However, the 15th-century ship atop the altar serves as a reminder of the city's seafaring heyday. ⓐ Pl. de Santa Maria ⓘ 933 102 390 ⓛ 09.00–13.30, 16.30–20.00 Mon–Sat, 10.00–13.00, 16.30–20.00 Sun ⓝ Metro: Jaume I

CULTURE

Museu d'Història de Catalunya (History Museum of Catalonia)

The Palau de Mar (Palace of the Sea), the port's old general warehouse, is a fine example of 19th-century industrial architecture. Nowadays, it contains the History Museum of Catalonia, a fascinating hands-on museum illustrating the great moments of the region's history and providing a valuable insight into Catalan lifestyle over the centuries. The museum café, on the top floor of the Palau de Mar, offers one of the best views of the city. ⓐ Palau de Mar, Pl. Pau Vila 3 ⓘ 932 254 700 ⓦ www.mhcat.net ⓛ 10.00–19.00 Tues & Thur–Sat, 10.00–20.00 Wed, 10.00–14.30 Sun ⓝ Metro: Barceloneta. Admission charge

Museu Picasso

Not only is this museum the city's greatest tourist attraction, but it is also the most important and most complete collection of early artworks by Pablo Picasso in the world. Although the great Spanish artist was born in Andalucía, he moved to Barcelona in 1895, when he was just 14 years old, and spent seven of his most formative years here.

The outstanding collection is housed in five adjoining medieval palaces on the beautiful Carrer Montcada. It traces Picasso's career from 1890 to 1904, from early childhood sketches and a range of styles from his time at La Lotja art school to the famous Blue Period. The collection then leaps to 1917 and the more mature, distinctive Cubism of later years, and demonstrates his versatility and extraordinary artistic development over the decades. ❸ C/ Montcada 15–23 ❶ 933 196 310 Ⓦ www.museupicasso.bcn.cat 🕐 10.00–20.00 Tues–Sun Ⓜ Metro: Jaume I. Admission charge

Museu de la Xocolata (Chocolate Museum)

A paradise for chocaholics, this attractive museum houses a fabulous collection of *mones* (elaborate chocolate sculptures) made by Barcelona's master chefs for the yearly Easter competition. The *mones* range from a hulking model of Floquet de Neu, the Zoo's deceased albino gorilla, to the windmill scene from Don Quijote or the chariot race from Ben Hur. There is also a brief history of cocoa and chocolate, a glass-fronted cookery workshop and, naturally, a wonderful chocolate shop. ❸ C/ Comerç 36 ❶ 932 687 878 Ⓦ www.museudelaxocolata.cat 🕐 10.00–19.00 Mon, Wed–Sat, 10.00–15.00 Sun Ⓜ Metro: Jaume I. Admission charge

Palau de la Música Catalana (Palace of Catalan Music)

This dazzling palace, built in the pure *Modernista* style by Domenech i Montaner in 1908, is considered one of the finest concert houses in the world. Each year it hosts some 300 concerts, with an attendance of over half a million people. In a city full of architectural wonders, it stands out as one of the greatest works of *Modernisme* and a symbol of the renaissance of Catalan culture. Indeed, in 1997 UNESCO declared it a World Heritage Site. If you have time, go to a concert – it's the best way to enjoy the building. ⓐ C/ Sant Pere Mès Alt ☎ 932 957 200 ⓦ www.palaumusica.org ⓛ Box office: 10.00–21.00; guided tours: 10.00–15.30 Ⓝ Metro: Urquinaona

RETAIL THERAPY

Alea Majoral Galería de Joyas Tiny boutique at the heart of La Ribera, showcasing up-and-coming Catalan and international jewellers. ⓐ C/ Argenteria 66 ☎ 933 101 373 ⓦ www.aleagaleria.com ⓛ 10.30–20.30 Mon–Fri, 11.00–20.30 Sat Ⓝ Metro: Jaume I or Barceloneta

Galeria Maeght A prestigious gallery of 20th-century art, design and photography. ⓐ C/ Montcada 25 (1st floor) ☎ 933 104 245 ⓦ www.maeght.com ⓛ 10.00–14.00, 16.00–19.00 Tues–Fri, 10.00–15.00 Sat Ⓝ Metro: Jaume I

Maremàgnum A huge waterfront leisure complex with numerous fashion boutiques including Calvin Klein, Mango, H&M, Quiksilver, Women's Secret and top Spanish designer, Adolfo Domínguez. ⓐ Moll d'Espanya ☎ 932 258 100 ⓦ www.maremagnum.es ⓛ 10.00–22.00 Ⓝ Metro: Barceloneta or Drassanes

Museu Picasso An excellent museum shop, brimming with Picasso-inspired souvenirs and gifts. ⓐ C/ Montcada 15

933 196 310 ⓦ www.museupicasso.bcn.es ⓛ 10.00–20.00
Tues–Sun Ⓜ Metro: Jaume I

On Land The quintessential Born boutique with a smattering
of sharp and sexy streetwear from local fashion heroes such as
Josep Font or Divinas Palabras. ⓐ C/ Princesa 25 ⓣ 933 100 211
ⓦ www.on-land.com ⓛ 17.00–20.30 Mon, 11.00–14.00, 17.00–20.30
Tues–Fri, 11.00–20.30 Sat Ⓜ Metro: Jaume I

TAKING A BREAK

Bubó £ ❶ Carles Mampel's sumptuous and intricately designed
pralines, sachertortes and petits fours make for a seriously classy
afternoon coffee. For savoury treats there's a tiny tapas bar next door.
ⓐ C/ Caputxes 10 ⓣ 932 687 224 ⓦ www.bubo.ws ⓛ 16.00–22.00
Mon, 10.00–22.00 Tues–Thur & Sun; 10.00–00.00 Fri & Sat
Ⓜ Metro: Jaume I

Buenas Migas £ ❷ A lively café with terrace tables overlooking the
sea, offering focaccia, pasta dishes, soups, salads and a great range
of homemade cakes and tarts. The name means 'Good Crumbs'.
ⓐ Pl. del Mar ⓣ 932 216 316 ⓦ www.buenasmigas.com ⓛ 10.00–00.00
Mon–Thur & Sun, 10.00–01.00 Fri & Sat, June–Sept; 10.00–23.00
Mon–Thur & Sun; 10.00–00.00 Fri & Sat, Oct–May Ⓜ Metro: Barceloneta

La Miranda del Museu £ ❸ You don't need to buy a ticket to the
museum to enjoy this little-known rooftop café and restaurant with the
most spectacular views over the port. Perfect for a coffee break on the
terrace or a good value set lunch. ⓐ Museu d'Història de Catalunya,
Pl. Pau Vila 3 ⓣ 932 255 007 ⓦ www.restaurantportinyol.com/museu

🕐 10.00–19.00 Tues, 10.00–20.00 Wed, 10.00–19.00, 21.00–23.00 Thur–Sat, 10.00–17.00 Sun Ⓜ Metro: Barceloneta

AFTER DARK

RESTAURANTS

Most people head to La Barceloneta to eat in its smart harbourside seafood restaurants – a prime location for paella and people-watching – while El Born and La Ribera are packed with fashionable bistros and brasseries.

Cuines Santa Caterina £ ❹ Set in the flashy new Santa Caterina market, this huge airy restaurant with wooden refectory-style tables serves up international fusion dishes, from tempura to traditional Catalan botifarra sausage. 🔢 Av. Francesc Cambó 16 ☎ 932 689 918 Ⓦ www.cuinessantacaterina.com 🕐 13.00–16.00, 20.00–23.00 Mon–Wed & Sun, 13.00–16.00, 20.00–00.30 Thur–Sat Ⓜ Metro: Jaume I

Euskal Etxea £ ❺ The best place in Barcelona to try *pintxos* (the Basque version of tapas), with an open buffet of exquisite little snacks speared on a slice of bread. The restaurant at the back serves heartier Basque specialities. 🔢 Placeta Montcada 1–3, near Passeig del Born ☎ 933 102 185 Ⓦ www.euskaletxeak.org 🕐 Bar: 19.00–00.00 Mon, 12.00–17.00, 19.00–00.00 Tues–Sat; restaurant: 20.30–23.30 Mon, 13.30–16.00, 20.30–23.30 Tues–Sat Ⓜ Metro: Jaume I

La Paradeta £ ❻ Excellent value seafood served up canteen style: queue to choose from piles of fresh clams, shrimp and fish on ice, tell them how you want it cooked and wait for your number to be

called. 🅐 C/ Comerç 7 🅣 932 681 939 🅦 www.laparadeta.com
🅛 20.00–23.30 Tues–Fri, 13.00–16.00, 20.00–00.00 Sat, 13.00–16.00
Sun Ⓝ Metro: Arc de Triomf

Cal Pep ££ ❼ A classic locals' restaurant specialising in seafood. Sit at
the bar and try some of the mouth-watering tapas. 🅐 Pl. de les Olles 8
🅣 933 107 961 🅛 20.00–23.45 Mon, 13.30–16.00, 20.00–23.45 Tues–Sat
🅦 www.calpep.com Ⓝ Metro: Barceloneta or Jaume I

Can Majó ££ ❽ One of Barceloneta's top seafood restaurants serves
up paella and piles of fresh lobster and langoustines just a stone's
throw from the beach. Book in advance for Sunday lunchtime.
🅐 C/ Almirall Aixada 23 🅣 932 215 455 🅦 www.canmajo.es
🅛 13.00–16.00, 20.00–23.30 Tues–Sat, 13.00–16.00 Sun
Ⓝ Metro: Barceloneta

Can Ramonet £££ ❾ A neighbourhood classic, this traditional fish
restaurant is housed in one of the oldest buildings in the Barceloneta.
Sit among huge wooden barrels to enjoy an aperitif or tuck into
mounds of fresh lobster on the shady terrace. 🅐 Plaça de la
Maquinista 17 🅣 933 193 064 🅛 12.00–00.00 Ⓝ Metro: Barceloneta

Comerç 24 £££ ❿ Avant-garde Catalan cuisine from Carles Abellan,
a protégé of Ferran Adrià. Enjoy a parade of tiny, eccentric dishes
in sharp and sexy surroundings. 🅐 C/ Comerç 24 🅣 933 192 102
🅦 www.comerc24.com 🅛 13.30–15.30, 20.30–23.00 Tues–Sat
Ⓝ Metro: Arc de Triomf

Hofmann £££ ⓫ Spain's top cookery school and the eponymous
restaurant of celebrity chef Mey Hofmann. Expect clever playful

dishes with especially interesting desserts such as a fruit pudding presented in an edible spun sugar jam jar. ⓐ C/ Argentería 74–8 ⓣ 933 195 889 ⓦ www.hofmann-bcn.com ⓛ 13.30–15.30, 21.00–23.15 Mon–Fri ⓝ Metro: Jaume I

BARS & CLUBS

CDLC The dance floor at Carpe Diem Lounge Club is surrounded by veiled white beds where the VIPs of Barcelona drink their expensive cocktails and try to spot all the other celebrities. ⓐ Passeig Marítim 32 ⓣ 932 240 470 ⓦ www.cdlcbarcelona.com ⓛ 10.00–03.00 ⓝ Metro: Ciutadella Vila Olímpica

Club Catwalk Right under the glamorous Hotel Arts, this swish club is where all the aspiring models go to preen and dance to R&B, house and hip-hop. ⓐ C/ Ramón Trias Fargas 2-4 ⓣ 932 216 161 ⓦ www.clubcatwalk.net ⓛ 00.00–05.30 Wed–Sun ⓝ Metro: Ciutadella Vila Olímpica

Le Kasbah An intimate Moroccan-style bar playing easy listening, minimal, house, funk, latin and jazz sounds. ⓐ Palau del Mar, Pl. Pau Vilà ⓣ 932 380 722 ⓦ www.ottozutz.com ⓛ 22.30–03.00 ⓝ Metro: Barceloneta

Razzmatazz Five different dance floors under one roof, each with different music genres and some of the city's top DJs. ⓐ C/ Almogàvers 122 ⓣ 933 208 200 ⓦ www.salarazzmatazz.com ⓛ 01.00–05.00 Fri & Sat ⓝ Metro: Marina

El Xampanyet A tiny champagne bar with blue-tiled walls, marble tables and a zinc bar, combining old-fashioned charm with a lively, young crowd. C/ Montcada 22 933 197 003 12.00–16.00, 19.00–23.30 Tues–Sat, 12.00–16.00 Sun Metro: Jaume I

CINEMA

IMAX Port Vell Think big with this giant wraparound 3D screen. Moll d'Espanya 932 251 111 www.imaxportvell.com Metro: Drassanes

Yelmo Icària Cineplex The 15 screens offer Hollywood blockbusters and mainstream Spanish releases, all in the original version with subtitles in Spanish. C/ Salvador Espriú 61 93 2 217 585 www.yelmocineplex.es Metro: Ciutadella Vila Olímpica

ENTERTAINMENT

This area contains one of the city's main concert venues, the Palau de la Música Catalana. There are also occasional concerts and recitals in the Basilica of Santa Maria del Mar (see page 79), and open-air theatre, concerts and dance events in Parc de la Ciutadella (see page 77) during summer.

Palau de la Música Catalana (Palace of Catalan Music) Undoubtedly the most spectacular venue for classical music in town, staging frequent concerts by the Cor de Cambra (Chamber Choir) del Palau de la Música, or by the amateur Orfeó Català choir, for whom the auditorium was originally built (see page 80). C/ Sant Pere Mès Alt 932 957 200 www.palaumusica.org Box office: 10.00–21.00; guided tours: 10.00–15.30 Metro: Urquinaona

△ The spectacular Palau de la Música Catalana

L'Eixample & Gràcia

L'Eixample (The Extension) was built between 1860 and 1920 to accommodate the burgeoning bourgeois population, and to merge the outlying villages of Sants, Sarrià-Sant Gervasi and Gràcia into the modern city. Its construction coincided with the emergence of Catalan *Modernisme*, and many of its wealthy new residents commissioned the great architects of the day to design grand mansions for them in this flamboyant new style. As a consequence, the district resembles a huge open-air museum, containing most of the city's greatest *Modernista* landmarks, including Gaudí's legendary Sagrada Família church, Casa Batlló and La Pedrera. Today the Eixample remains a wealthy district, brimming with designer boutiques, smart hotels, sophisticated bars and restaurants.

To the north, the 'village' of Gràcia has long been known as a radical centre of Catalanism and, despite being completely engulfed by the city these days, the district still maintains a village atmosphere and the locals consider themselves Graciencs rather than Barcelonans.

CERDÀ'S EIXAMPLE
Ildefons Cerdà's geometric grid design for the Eixample was an innovative plan in its day, which broke completely with former models of Spanish urban planning. It divided the city into 550 symmetrical blocks covering an area of 23 sq km (9 sq miles), with the aptly named Avinguda Diagonal cutting through the blocks at a 45° angle to add a touch of quirkiness.

L'Eixample & Gràcia

0 — 500 metres
0 — 500 yards

Tibidabo ▲

VALLCARCA

Parc Güell

Casa Museu Gaudí

ST GERVASI

Vallcarca Ⓜ

CARRER DE LA MURTRA

CARRER DE L'HOSPITAL MILITAR

CARRER D'ESCIPIÓ

C DE PÀDUA

PLAÇA DE SANT JOAQUIM

Lesseps Ⓜ

CARRETERA DEL CARMEL

CARRER D'OLOT

EL CARMEL

C DE MÜLER

CARRER DE SANT SALVADOR

C DE BALCELLS

CARRER DE FRANÇA

CARRER DE PÀDUA

CARRER DE PRAGA

Parc del Guinardó

CARRER DE LA CABÈNIA

C DE RIOS ROSSAS

CARRER DE SANJOANISTES

TRAVESSERA DE DALT

C DE NIL FABRA

Casa Vicens

C DE LARRAR

CARRER DE LES CAMÈLIES

C DE BALMES

AVINGUDA DEL PRÍNCEP D'ASTÚRIES

Fontana Ⓜ

TRAVESSERA DE SANT ANTONI

GRÀCIA

C DE VIADA

CARRER DE MARTÍ

C DE MARTÍ

Parc de les Aigües

CARRER DE FRANCESC ALEGRE

PLAÇA DE LA VIRREINA

C DE L'OR

Alfons X Ⓜ

Guinardó Ⓜ

C DE LA GRANADA DEL PENEDÉS

CARRER DE TEROL

CARRER DE RAMÓN Y CAJAL

CARRER GRAN DE GRÀCIA

C DE MOZART

CARRER DE ST LLUIS

L'ENCARNACIÓ

CARRER DEL MAS CASANOVES

RIERA DE SANT MIQUEL

❸

❽

& Luz de Gas

VIA AUGUSTA

TRAVESSERA DE GRÀCIA

Joanic Ⓜ

BAILÈN

CARRER DEL PARELALÈNEZ

Jardins Príncep de Girona

Hospital de la Santa Creu i de Sant Pau ✚

C DE LA FRATERNITAT

CARRER DE SANT ANTONI MARIA CLARET

Jardins La Sedeta

Jardins Indústria

Hospital de Sant Pau ✚

C DE BONAVISTA

C STA EULALIA

CARRER DE ROGER DE FLOR

CARRER DE LA INDÚSTRIA

LA SAGRADA FAMÍLIA

CARRER DE CÓRSEGA

Diagonal Ⓜ

AVINGUDA DIAGONAL

Museu de la Música

CARRER DEL ROSSELLÓ

❼

Sagrada Família Ⓜ

AVINGUDA DE GAUDÍ

CARRER DE CÓRSEGA

Casa Milà 'La Pedrera' ❷

CARRER DE PROVENÇA

Verdaguer Ⓜ

CARRER DE PROVENÇA

PLAÇA DE LA SAGRADA FAMÍLIA

CASTILLEJOS

C DE DOS DE MAIG

Museu Egipci de Barcelona

C DE MALLORCA

PLAÇA MOSSÈN JACINT VERDAGUER

Temple Expiatori de la Sagrada Família

C DE MALLORCA

Fundació Antoni Tàpies

Casa Batlló ❹

Casa Amatller

CARRER DE VALÈNCIA

AVINGUDA DIAGONAL

CARRER DE VALÈNCIA

Encants Ⓜ

Manzana de la Discordia

CARRER D'ARAGÓ

CARRER DE ROGER DE FLOR

DIAGONAL

CARRER D'ARAGÓ

CARRER DELS ENAMORATS

Lleó-Morera

CARRER DEL CONSELL DE CENT

❻ Girona Ⓜ

DRETA DE L'EIXAMPLE

Esc Universitat de Treball Social

Estació Passeig de Gràcia

CARRER DE LA DIPUTACIÓ

Monumental Ⓜ

PLAÇA DE LES GLÒRIES CATALANES

Passeig de Gràcia Ⓜ

GRAN VIA DE LES CORTS CATALANES

Tetuan Ⓜ

Plaça de Toros Monumental

Glòries Ⓜ

❶❺ & Urgell

Catalunya Ⓜ

ⓘ

CARRER DE GIRONA

CARRER DE BAILÈN

CARRER DE CASP

CARRER DE SICÍLIA

CARLES I

Teatro Nacional de Catalunya

PLAÇA DE CATALUNYA

Urquinaona Ⓜ

RONDA DE SANT PERE

EL FORT PIUS

CARRER D'AUSIÀS MARC

CARRER DE RIBES

AVDA MERIDIANA

L'Auditori & Museu de la Música

LA RAMBLA

VIA LAIETANA

CARRER ORTIGOSA DE TRAFALGAR

CARRER D'ALÍ BEI

Arc de Triomf Ⓜ

Barcelona Nord

PASSEIG DE SANT JOAN

C DE BOLÍVIA

CARRER DE TÀNGER

Arc de Triomf

AVENUE DE VILANOVA

Marina Ⓜ

SIGHTS & ATTRACTIONS

Casa Milà – 'La Pedrera' (Milà House – 'The Stone Quarry')

Gaudí was at the peak of his architectural career when he constructed the extraordinary apartment block of Casa Milà for dilettante politician Pere Milà in 1912. It was Gaudí's last and most famous secular building, and also one of his most inventive – a triumph of aesthetics over practicality, built entirely on columns and arches, with sinuous lines and rippling limestone façades, supposedly without a single straight line or right-angled corner. Every last detail is intricately designed, right down to the crooked banisters, ergonomic doorknobs, balconies of recycled wrought-ironwork and ceramic-encrusted chimneys of the roof terrace.

Sadly, soon after its construction, Casa Milà was to become Spain's most controversial apartment block. Its innovative appearance so shocked Barcelonans when it was built that they nicknamed it 'La Pedrera' ('The Stone Quarry'). After years of neglect, it was eventually declared a World Heritage Site by UNESCO in 1984 (the first 20th-century building to achieve the honour) and, ironically, it is now one of the city's most admired buildings.

Inside the building is the fascinating Espai Gaudí, an exhibition about the origins and construction of Casa Milà, with drawings, models, photographs and audiovisuals. But the highlight of any visit is undoubtedly the extraordinary undulating roof with its strangely shaped chimney stacks and amazing bird's-eye vistas of the Eixample. During summer weekends, the roof terrace is the spectacular venue for *La Pedrera de Nit*, a series of open-air evening concerts. ⓐ Passeig de Gràcia 92 ⓣ 902 400 973 ⓦ www.caixacatalunya.cat/obrasocial ⓛ 09.00–18.30 Jan & Dec; 09.00–20.00 Feb–Nov ⓜ Metro: Diagonal. Admission charge

🔺 Modernista *architecture in L'Eixample*

Hospital de la Santa Creu i de Sant Pau

This beautiful unusual hospital complex forms one of Europe's finest ensembles of Modernism, designed by the innovative architect Domènech i Montaner. Not only did he defy the orderliness of the Eixample by aligning the buildings at 45° to the street grid, but he also broke with the tradition of having one large hospital building, by creating a 'hospital-village' of 18 small pavilions, connected by a series of underground passages. Construction began in 1902 and, when the hospital was eventually inaugurated in 1930, it was considered to be

MANZANA DE LA DISCORDIA

The most impressive block on the Passeig de Gràcia (between Carrer d'Aragó and Carrer Consell de Cent) is called the Manzana de la Discordia (Block of Discord), because of the clashing architectural styles of Casa Amatller, Casa Batlló and Casa Lleó-Morera (see below) – three of the most celebrated architectural ensembles and a magnificent showcase for the city's greatest exponents of *Modernisme*, Montaner, Cadafalch and Gaudí. View them by day and by night, when their façades are magically lit.

one of the most advanced in Europe. It ceased to function as a working hospital in 2006 due to the demands of modern-day medicine and is now mainly used for research, although it may eventually become a museum of *Modernisme*. The entire complex is protected as a UNESCO World Heritage Site. ⓐ C/ de Sant Antoni María Claret 167 ⓣ 932 919 000 ⓦ www.santpau.es ⓛ Grounds: 24 hrs; tours: by reservation 10.00 & 12.00 ⓝ Metro: Hospital de Sant Pau

Manzana de la Discordia

The most celebrated city block or *manzana* ('apple', named after the round shape of the blocks in the Eixample, due to their chamfered corners) of 'discord' contains three clashing *Modernista* masterpieces. Heading uphill towards Tibidabo, the first is the white, neo-Gothic wedding cake fantasy of the Casa Lleó Morera (1902-5) by Lluís Domènech i Montaner. It stands out for its sumptuous stonework and cupola. At number 41 stands the Casa Amatller (1900), designed by Josep Puig i Cadfalch for a local chocolate magnate; look out for the unusual stepped Flemish gable and cheeky stone figures carved around the doorway. The building currently houses the Centre del Modernisme, which provides information and multilingual guides on the Ruta del Modernisme (see page 20).

The most photographed of them all is next door at number 43: Antoni Gaudí's masterful **Casa Batlló** (☏ 932 160 306 ⓦ www.casabatllo.cat ⏰ 09.00–20.00. Admission charge), whose sinuous curves stand in stark contrast to its geometric neighbour. The dazzling polychrome façade, tibia-like stone columns and

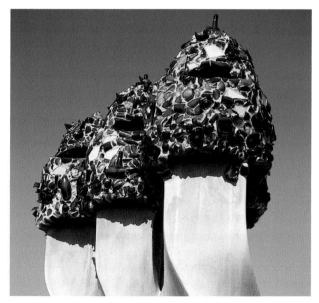

🔺 *Rooftop chimneys at Casa Milù 'Lu Pedrera'*

humped scaly roof are said to represent the triumph of St George over the dragon (see page 12). An audio-guided tour of the extraordinary interior, and the rooftop with its unique chimneys, reveals Gaudí's unparalleled freedom of imagination and abstract genius. ⓐ Passeig de Gràcia 35–43, Casa Batlló 43 ⓥ Metro: Passeig de Gràcia

Park Güell

The wealthy Güell family commissioned a number of works from Antoni Gaudí over the years, including Palau Güell (see page 107) and this eccentric hilltop park high up above the district of Gràcia. Sadly, Eusebi Güell's plan to create a residential garden city here, with 60 houses set in formal gardens, never came to fruition and the park was deemed a failure in its day. Only two houses were built, including the one where Gaudí briefly lived (now the Casa Museu Gaudí, containing a small but moving selection of his personal artefacts, wrought-ironwork and items of furniture).

Today, Park Güell is considered one of the city's treasures, outstanding for its clever fusion of architectural elements into the landscaping. In 1969, it was declared a national monument. Throughout its 20 hectares (49 acres), there are surreal sculptures, steps, bridges, and paths raised on columns of 'dripping' stonework. The main entrance is especially impressive, with massive wrought-iron gates, flanked by two oval pavilions with colourful mosaic domes. From here, a grand stairway, ornamented by a mosaic salamander fountain, leads to the Sala Hipòstila, a vast cavernous space originally intended as the marketplace. Its circular rooftop plaza, supported by 86 fluted columns, is edged with a curved continuous bench covered in multi-coloured *trencadís* (broken ceramics). The plaza affords far-reaching city vistas and makes an ideal picnic spot. ⓐ Musuem: Carretera del Carmel; park: C/ d'Olot ⓣ Museum: 932 193 811; park:

932 130 488 🕒 Museum: 10.00–17.45 Nov–Mar; 10.00–19.45 Apr–Oct; park: 10.00–dusk 🚌 Bus: 24; metro: Vallcarca, then ten-minute walk. Admission charge for museum

Passeig de Gràcia

This broad leafy boulevard forms the axis of Cerdà's plan for the Eixample (see feature box on page 88) and is considered to be the 'Champs-Élysées of Catalonia'. It was constructed in 1827 on the path that once joined Barcelona to the village of Gràcia, and today its

🔺 *Tip-top detail at La Sagrada Família*

central tree-lined pedestrian walkway forms a northern extension of La Rambla (see page 63). By the turn of the 20th century, it was one of the most sought-after residential streets, flanked by some of the city's most elegant and striking mansions. Other special features include the unusual Gaudíesque 'bench and lamppost' ensembles. It was not until the 1920s that the boulevard became a major shopping thoroughfare. Ⓝ Metro: Passeig de Gràcia

Plaça de Catalunya

This busy square is the nerve-centre of Barcelona, at the confluence of many major thoroughfares: La Rambla and Avinguda Portal de l'Àngel to the south; Passeig de Gràcia and La Rambla de Catalunya to the north. The square adopted its final form in the 1920s, when an extensive esplanade joined the Old Town with the Eixample, and the square replaced Plaça de Sant Jaume as the heart of Barcelona. Today, with its sculptures and symmetrical fountains, it is a central meeting point for Barcelonans.

Temple Expiatori de la Sagrada Família (Expiatory Temple of the Holy Family)

This extraordinary building is surely the most unusual temple in the world, and Barcelona's most distinctive landmark. It also represents the synthesis of architectural genius Antoni Gaudí's work. The first stone was laid in 1882 and the devout Catholic worked on the project for over 40 years. Such was his commitment to the building, he even lived in an on-site workshop studio for the last 15 years of his life. His dream was to create Europe's biggest temple and a bible in stone, with three façades representing the birth, death and resurrection of Christ, and 18 mosaic-clad domes and pinnacles to symbolise the 12 Apostles, the four Evangelists, the Virgin Mary and Christ.

Following his untimely death in 1926 (see page 13), only the crypt, the majority of the Nativity façade, the apse and just four towers were complete, and his plans for the rest of the building were uncertain after blueprints were destroyed by anarchists in the Civil War. After his death, there was great controversy as to whether or not the work should resume. Since 1952 the Passion façade has been added and there are now eight completed towers, each over 100 m (325 ft) tall. There is a museum in the crypt, documenting the past, present and future of Gaudí's monumental, unfinished cathedral through photographs, plans, audiovisuals and original sketches, together with decorative items and maquettes of his life's work in general.

The entrance ticket includes admission to the building work in progress, the museum and access to the multi-coloured towers, either on foot or by lift, for breathtaking views of the city. The Nativity façade – devoted to the birth and early life of Christ with three doors representing Faith, Hope and Charity – is best viewed from the small park in Plaça Gaudí. The detail of sculpture on the façade is truly extraordinary, depicting almost 100 species of plants and as many types of animals, including Gaudí's beloved chameleons, which can be seen carved into the stonework all over the cathedral. By contrast, the post-Gaudí Passion façade, completed in 1990 by sculptor Josep Maria Subirachs, is more angular, minimalist and contemporary, signifying the pain and sacrifice of the final part of Christ's life. The main façade of the basilica, devoted to the Celestial Glory, is now well under way.

It is estimated that there are a further 80 years of work, including the destruction of an entire block of apartments in front of the Glory façade to create an entrance avenue. Matters will not be speeded up by the subterranean construction of the AVE high-speed train line next to the temple. Nevertheless, the Sagrada Família remains one of the great architectural wonders of the world and a must-see

for every visitor to the city. ⓐ Pl. de la Sagrada Família (temple);
C/ Mallorca 401 (museum) ⓣ 932 073 031 ⓦ www.sagradafamilia.org
ⓛ 09.00–18.00 Oct–Mar; 09.00–20.00 Apr–Sept ⓜ Metro: Sagrada
Família. Admission charge

ⓞ The curvaceous main entrance to Park Güell

CULTURE

Fundació Antoni Tàpies (Antoni Tàpies Foundation)

Catalan artist Antoni Tàpies founded the Tàpies Foundation in 1984 to promote the study and understanding of modern art. It contains a specialist library, which documents art and artists of the 20th century, and one of the most extensive collections of Tàpies' own paintings, drawings and sculptures. It also hosts temporary exhibitions of contemporary art and culture. **ⓐ** C/ d'Aragó 255 **ⓣ** 934 870 315 **ⓦ** www.fundaciotapies.org **ⓛ** 10.00–20.00 Tues–Sun **ⓝ** Metro: Passeig de Gràcia. Admission charge

Museu Egipci de Barcelona (Egyptian Museum of Barcelona)

An outstanding collection of artefacts from Ancient Egypt owned by Egyptologist and hotelier Jordi Clos. Exhibits include everything from copper mirrors to an amazingly intact 5,000-year-old bed, mummified animals, infant sarcophagi and the wonderful statue of Osiris breastfeeding her son Horus. Book ahead on Friday and Saturday nights to see dramatic reconstructions of themes such as the life of Cleopatra or the mummification ritual. **ⓐ** C/ València 284 **ⓣ** 934 880 188 **ⓦ** www.museuegipci.com **ⓛ** 10.00–20.00 Mon–Sat, 10.00–14.00 Sun **ⓝ** Metro: Passeig de Gràcia. Admission charge

Museu de la Música (Music Museum)

The city music museum relocated to L'Auditori arts complex (see page 103) in 2007. Beautifully displayed in sleek, modern surroundings are some 500 instruments ranging from harps and violins to Lebanese derbekkahs and a full range of castanets and the Catalan flabiol (a type of recorder). There's a wealth of documents, such as letters from cellist Pau Casals and original sheet music by

composer Enric Granados, sound recordings and even an interactive space where visitors can try out instruments for themselves.
ⓐ C/ Lepant 150 ⓣ 932 563 650 ⓦ www.museumusica.bcn.cat
ⓛ 11.00–21.00 Mon & Wed–Fri, 10.00–19.00 Sat & Sun ⓝ Metro: Marina. Admission charge

RETAIL THERAPY

Adolfo Domínguez One of Spain's top menswear designers, famed for making linen suits popular with the slogan 'wrinkles are beautiful'.
ⓐ Passeig de Gràcia 89 ⓣ 934 874 889 ⓦ www.adolfo-dominguez.com
ⓛ 10.30–20.30 Mon–Sat ⓝ Metro: Passeig de Gràcia

Antonio Miró A local designer, celebrated worldwide for his shoes, specs, furnishings and sombre fashions. ⓐ C/ Consell de Cent 349
ⓣ 934 870 670 ⓦ www.antoniomiro.es ⓛ 10.30–20.30 Mon–Sat
ⓝ Metro: Passeig de Gràcia

Bagués One of the world's leading *Modernista* jewellers, housed in Casa Amatller. ⓐ Passeig de Gràcia 41 ⓣ 932 160 174 ⓦ www.bagues.com
ⓛ 10.00–20.30 Mon–Fri, 10.00–13.30, 17.00–20.30 Sat ⓝ Metro: Passeig de Gràcia

Bulevard dels Antiquaris A wonderful mall with some 70 shops specialising in oil paintings, jewellery, dolls, furniture and limited edition Tàpies and Miró prints. ⓐ Passeig de Gràcia 55 ⓣ 932 154 499
ⓦ www.bulevarddelsantiquaris.com ⓛ 10.30–13.30, 16.30–20.30
Mon–Sat ⓝ Metro: Passeig de Gràcia

Camper Catalonia's most famous footwear: colourful, almost childish

designs in exquisitely soft leather with the trademark recycled soles.
ⓐ C/ Pelai 13 ⓣ 933 024 124 ⓦ www.camper.com ⓛ 10.00–22.00
Mon–Sat ⓝ Metro: Cataluyna

Dos i Una Barcelona's first design shop is full of state-of-the-art
gadgetry and amusing gift ideas. ⓐ C/ Rosselló 275 ⓣ 932 177 032
ⓛ 10.30–14.00, 17.00–20.30 Mon–Sat ⓝ Metro: Diagonal

Muxart Fantastic creations by flamboyant Barcelonan shoe
designer, Hermenegildo Muxart. ⓐ C/ Rosselló 230 ⓣ 934 881 064
ⓦ www.muxart.com ⓛ 10.00–14.00, 16.30–20.20 Mon–Fri,
10.00–14.00 17.00–20.30 Sat ⓝ Metro: Provença or Diagonal

Vinçon An über-trendy home design store in the beautiful *Modernista*
mansion where artist Ramon Casas once lived. ⓐ Passeig de Gracià 96
ⓣ 932 156 050 ⓦ www.vincon.com ⓛ 10.00–20.30 Mon–Sat
ⓝ Metro: Passeig de Gracià

TAKING A BREAK

Bodega Sepúlveda £ ❶ The speciality at this genuine locals' bar
is *boquerons* (fresh anchovies). ⓐ C/ Sepúlveda 173 ⓣ 933 235 944
ⓦ www.bodegasepulveda.net ⓛ 13.30–16.30, 20.00–01.00 Mon–Fri,
20.00–01.00 Sat ⓝ Metro: Universitat

Bar Mut ££ ❷ An upmarket bar that retains its original
Modernista décor. Delectable seafood tapas are nibbled with
a glass of the eponymous vermouth. ⓐ C/ Pau Claris 192
ⓣ 932 174 338 ⓛ 09.00–00.00 Mon–Fri, 11.30–00.00 Sat & Sun
ⓝ Metro: Diagonal

Flash Flash Tortillería ££ ❸ *Tortillas* (omelettes) in 70 varieties and salads – perfect for a light lunch in monochrome seventies surroundings. ❸ C/ Granada del Penedès 25 ❶ 932 370 990 Ⓦ www.flashflashtortilleria.com ❶ 13.30–01.30 Ⓜ Metro: Diagonal

AFTER DARK

RESTAURANTS
El Glop de la Rambla £ ❹ Popular, affordable restaurant serving grilled meat dishes and local wines. ❸ La Rambla de Catalunya 65 ❶ 934 870 097 Ⓦ www.elglopdelarambla.com ❶ 13.00–16.00, 20.00–00.00 (until 01.00 Fri & Sat) Ⓜ Metro: Passeig de Gràcia

Inopia ££ ❺ The latest tapas sensation comes from Albert Adrià, brother to the world-famous Ferran. There's no culinary trickery here though, just perfectly executed versions of classic tapas served in bright, modern décor. ❸ C/ Tamarit 104 ❶ 934 245 231 Ⓦ www.barinopia.com ❶ 19.00–00.00 Mon–Fri, 13.00–15.30 19.00–00.00 Sat Ⓜ Metro: Poble Sec

Noti ££ ❻ Creative Spanish-Italian cuisine in a sleek, urban interior – a popular choice for business lunches. ❸ C/ Roger de Llúria 35 ❶ 933 426 673 Ⓦ www.noti-universal.com ❶ 13.30–16.00, 20.30–00.00 Mon–Fri, 20.30–00.00 Sat Ⓜ Metro: Passeig de Gràcia

Alkimia £££ ❼ The Michelin star makes booking ahead essential but these gourmet versions of classic Spanish dishes are well worth the trouble. One of the most desirable tables in town. ❸ C/ Indústria 79 ❶ 932 076 115 ❶ 13.30–15.30, 20.30–23.00 Mon–Fri Ⓜ Metro: Joanic

Saüc £££ ❽ An unmissable experience for anyone serious about food, the 'elderberry' has a surprisingly affordable set lunch and highly accomplished takes on Catalan classics. Book well ahead. ⓐ Passatge Lluis Pellicer 12 ❶ 933 210 189 Ⓦ www.saucrestaurant.com ❶ 13.30–15.30, 20.30–22.30 Tues–Sat Ⓝ Metro: Hospital Clínic

BARS, CLUBS & LIVE MUSIC

Antilla BCN Latin Club The best salsateca in town has dance classes, live music concerts and the full range of Latin flavours from *merengue* to *son*. ⓐ C/ Aragó 141 ❶ 934 514 564 Ⓦ www.antillasalsa.com ❶ 23.00–03.30 Mon–Wed & Sun, 23.00–04.00 Fri & Sat Ⓝ Metro: Urgell

Buda Restaurante One of the Eixample's most glamorous nightspots with gilded furniture and chandeliers lighting models' cheekbones to perfection. Every night has a theme, from Geisha to Bollywood. ⓐ C/ Pau Claris 92 ❶ 933 184 252 Ⓦ www.budarestaurante.com ❶ 21.00–03.00 Ⓝ Metro: Catalunya

Luz de Gas A beautiful old music hall with plenty of swagged red velvet and tasselled lamps. Nightly concerts start at 23.30 and range in style from blues to Spanish rock. ⓐ C/ Muntaner 246 ❶ 932 097 711 Ⓦ www.luzdegas.com ❶ 01.00–05.30 Ⓝ FGC: Muntaner. Admission charge

THEATRE, MUSIC & DANCE

L'Auditori This modern arts complex is home to the National Catalan Orchestra and stages orchestral concerts as well as recitals in its two theatres. ⓐ C/ Lepant 150 ❶ 932 479 300 Ⓦ www.auditori.cat Ⓝ Metro: Marina

Montjuïc & El Raval

South of the city, the vast hill of Montjuïc is named 'Mountain of the Jews' after an early Jewish necropolis here. In 1929 it was the venue for the International Expo, and in 1992 it was the main site of the Barcelona Olympics. Today, with its top-notch sports facilities, together with some of the city's finest museums and galleries, it is a popular place for both locals and visitors at weekends. On the lower slopes of Montjuïc, the up-and-coming residential *barri* (quarter) of Poble Sec was once so poor it didn't even have a water supply, hence its name – 'Dry Village'. It joins the lively district of El Raval, also known as Barri Xinès (China Town), formerly a run-down area renowned as a centre of drugs, crime and prostitution. Nowadays, the upper part of the Raval has tidied up its act and, thanks to the opening of such institutions as the Museum of Contemporary Art (MACBA) and the neighbouring Contemporary Cultural Centre (CCCB), it is becoming newly fashionable, filled with galleries, fashion boutiques and chic cafés.

SIGHTS & ATTRACTIONS

L'Anella Olímpica & Museu Olímpic i de l'Esport (The Olympic Ring & Museum of Olympics & Sport)

Santiago Calatrava's space-age communications tower dominates the skyline on Montjuïc hill. It marks the Olympic Ring – a monumental sports complex of concrete and marble, which served, in 1992, as the main venue for the Olympic Games. The Estadi Olímpic (Olympic Stadium) was originally designed in 1936 as an alternative venue to the Nazis' infamous Berlin Games. Today, highlights of the 1992 Games can be relived though memorabilia and video clips in the Olympics & Sport museum situated beneath the stadium, which

⬤ *The striking Torre de Calatrava at l'Anella Olímpica*

also has sporting artefacts such as Miguel Induraín's bicycle and virtual enactments of performances, such as Bob Beamon's winning long jump. Also open to the public are the Picornell outdoor swimming pool and the state-of-the-art domed Palau Sant Jordi, which looks more like a UFO than an indoor sports arena. Museum: ⓐ Av. de l'Estadi 60 ⓘ 932 925 379 ⓦ www.fundaciobarcelonaolimpica.es ⓛ 10.00–20.00 Mon & Wed–Sat, 10.00–14.30 Sun, Apr–Sept; 10.00–18.00 Mon & Wed–Sat, 10.00–14.30 Sun, Oct–Mar ⓝ Bus: 50, 55, 61. Admission charge

Castell de Montjuïc (Montjuïc Castle)

This imposing 17th-century fortress, standing on the bluff of Montjuïc hill, has a dark history as a prison and place of execution and torture in the Civil War, and was even used to bombard restless citizens into submission by Isabel II in 1842. It used to house a military museum but is currently being converted into a Centre for Peace Studies. It is not open to the public. ⓐ Ctra de Montjuïc 66 ⓝ Metro: Paral.lel, then Funicular de Montjuïc; bus: 50

Palau Güell (Güell Palace)

This eccentric building, constructed in the 1880s and reopened in summer 2007 after extensive renovation, was Antoni Gaudí's first major architectural project. It was commissioned by the affluent industrialist Eusebi Güell, who shocked society by announcing he wished to move into C/ Nou de la Rambla, on the fringe of El Raval's notorious red-light district, rather than the fashionable new Eixample district, in order to be near his parents' home on La Rambla. Given the seedy neighbourhood, Gaudí created an austere façade resembling a fortress, with battlements, grilles like portcullises and wrought-iron dragons to fend off unwanted visitors.

The interior is lavishly decorated and fascinating. Follow the one-hour guided tour down to the cavernous basement stables, through various rooms decorated with *Modernista* furniture and fittings of wrought-iron, glass, ceramics and wood, and up to the rooftop terrace – an extraordinary forest of quirky finials and chimneys, decorated with coloured *trencadís* mosaics (broken ceramic pieces) and glass. The Güell family did not live here long as the palace was confiscated by Spanish Civil War anarchists in 1936, who used it as their military headquarters and prison. Today, it is protected as a UNESCO World Heritage Site. Renovation work is ongoing until 2010 or beyond, but visitors can still see the underground stables, ground floor and a short video about the building. Admission is free during the renovation period. ⓐ C/ Nou de la Rambla 3 ⓣ 933 173 974 ⓦ www.palauguell.cat ⓛ 10.00–14.30 Tues–Sat ⓜ Metro: Drassanes

Pavelló Mies van der Rohe (Mies van der Rohe Pavilion)

This masterpiece of modern rationalist design was created on the lower slopes of Montjuïc hill as the German Pavilion for the 1929 International Expo by the celebrated Bauhaus architect Ludwig Mies van der Rohe. It was dismantled at the end of the fair and subsequently reconstructed in the 1980s to commemorate the centenary of his birth. It is a construction of astonishing simplicity, combining marble, onyx, glass, chrome and water using simple geometrical forms and clean lines. Its ultra-minimalist functional interior contains an exhibition on the architect's life and work, and includes his famous square-shaped leather and steel 'Barcelona Chair', created especially for the exhibition, which has since become an icon of modern design. ⓐ Av. del Marquès de Comillas, Montjuïc ⓣ 934 234 016 ⓦ www.miesbcn.com ⓛ 10.00–20.00 ⓜ Metro: Espanya; bus: 13, 50, 100. Admission charge

Plaça d'Espanya

This bustling square and major traffic intersection was originally designed as a grand entrance to the 1929 Universal Exposition. The square itself is dominated by a classical-style monument designed by Gaudí's right-hand man, Josep Maria Jujol, and representing the three great rivers of Spain. The unusual Moorish-style building on one corner is the former bullring of Les Arenes, now converted into an ultra-modern leisure centre designed by Richard Rogers and known as the 'piazza in the sky'. It backs onto the recently renovated Parc Joan Miró (Joan Miró Park), with its startling 22 m (72 ft) high mosaic sculpture entitled *Dona i Ocell* (Woman and Bird).

Back in Plaça d'Espanya, a series of staircases, fountains and outdoor escalators leads you towards the impressive Palau Nacional and MNAC (see page 114). But the real crowd-puller is La Font Màgica (The Magic Fountain), which lies on Plaça Carles Buïgas just up the steps from Plaça d'Espanya and puts on free illuminated musical fountain displays. ❶ 933 161 000 ⏰ Fountain displays every 30 mins 21.30–23.00 Thur–Sun, May–Sept; 19.00–20.30 Fri & Sat, Oct–Apr Ⓜ Metro: Espanya

CULTURE

CaixaForum

The cultural nerve centre of Catalonia's biggest savings bank, La Caixa, lays on some of the best temporary art exhibitions in the whole city, ranging from photography to fine art, monographs to sculpture. No expense has been spared with the building either: the site was originally an enormous red brick textile factory built in grand industrial *Modernista* style by Josep Puig i Cadafalch in 1911; having fallen into dereliction by the end of the last century, La Caixa paid for its complete

renovation, adding a white marble entrance plaza by Arata Isozaki, a striking Sol LeWitt mural, a 350-seater auditorium for cultural performances and a library. ⓐ Casaramona, Av. Marquès de Comillas 6–8 ⓣ 934 768 600 ⓦ www.fundacio.lacaixa.es ⓛ 10.00–20.00 Mon–Fri & Sun, 10.00–22.00 Sat ⓜ Metro: Espanya

Fundació Joan Miró (Joan Miró Foundation)

Fundació Joan Miró, on Montjuïc hill, pays homage to one of Barcelona's greatest artists. Famous for his childlike style and use of vivid primary colours, his work captures the very essence of this vibrant Mediterranean city. Miró was born in Barcelona in 1893 and spent much of his life here, developing his bold style and use of bright vibrant colours. The gallery, itself a work of art designed by Josep Lluís Sert, is a beautiful modern building of airy white spaces, massive windows and skylights set in gardens overlooking the city – and a perfect backdrop for 240 paintings, 175 sculptures, around 8,000 drawings, nine tapestries, four ceramics and his complete graphic works – the most complete collection of Miró's work in the world, many of which were donated to the Foundation by Miró himself.

The Foundation also stages temporary exhibitions of modern art, contemporary music recitals and a special permanent exhibition entitled 'To Joan Miró', including works by Calder, Ernst, Tàpies, Moore, Matisse and others, given to the Foundation in memory of the great Catalan surrealist. ⓐ Parc de Montjuïc ⓣ 934 439 470 ⓦ www.fundaciomiro-bcn.org ⓛ 10.00–19.00 Tues–Sat (until 21.00 Thur), 10.00–14.30 Sun, Oct–June; 10.00–20.00 Tues–Sat (until 21.30 Thur), 10.00–14.30 Sun, July–Sept ⓜ Metro: Paral.lel then Funicular de Montjuïc; bus: 61. Admission charge

◖ *Sculpture – and a great view – at the Fundació Joan Miró*

Museu d'Art Contemporani de Barcelona – MACBA (Museum of Contemporary Art)

Hidden among the shabby narrow back streets in El Raval, this dazzling white glass-fronted museum comes as a something of a surprise, towering over the stark concrete Plaça dels Àngels. The dramatic building, with its swooping ramps, white-on-white décor and glass-walled galleries designed by American architect Richard Meier, was initially the subject of much controversy and almost upstages the art installations it contains. Nonetheless, it is regarded as one of the city's must-see galleries, focusing on the art movements of the second half of the 20th century, with special emphasis on Catalan and Spanish artists. Its extensive collection is exhibited in rotation, with works by Klee, Tàpies, Miró, Calder and Hurst among others. It also hosts temporary contemporary art exhibitions.

ⓐ Pl. dels Àngels 1 ⓣ 934 120 810 ⓦ www.macba.es ⓛ 11.00–19.30 Mon & Wed–Fri, 10.00–20.00 Sat, 10.00–15.00 Sun ⓜ Metro: Catalunya. Admission charge

Museu Marítim (Maritime Museum)

The Maritime Museum is housed in the magnificent Drassanes Reials (Royal Shipyards), the largest and most complete medieval dockyards in the world. These impressive boatyards were built in the 13th century, at the height of Catalonia's maritime power, and are a triumph of Gothic civic architecture. Maps, charts, compasses, paintings, model ships, figureheads and countless other treasures of Barcelona's lengthy seafaring past fill their vast, church-like, stone-vaulted halls, and there are polyglot audio-guides to steer visitors around the key attractions.

Numerous boats are also on show, from the gold-medal-winning Flying Dutchman sloop raced by the Spanish sailing team at the

Barcelona Olympics to a 60 m (197 ft) replica of the royal galley *La Real*, flagship of Don Juan of Austria, which forms part of an exciting 45-minute multimedia spectacle 'The Great Sea Adventure'. The museum's flagship, the early 20th-century three-masted schooner *Santa Eulàlia* (renamed in honour of Barcelona's patron saint), is moored at the wooden pier at Barcelona's old port and is now also open to the public. ❸ Av. de les Drassanes ❶ 933 429 920 ⓦ www.museumaritimbarcelona.com ❻ 10.00–19.00 Ⓜ Metro: Drassanes. Admission charge

🔺 *The dramatic Museu d'Art Contemporani de Barcelona*

Museu Nacional d'Art de Catalunya – MNAC
(National Art Museum of Catalonia)

The staggering collections of the MNAC span a thousand years of
Catalan art, from the 10th to the 20th centuries. They are housed
in an imposing neoclassical palace, the Palau Nacional. Originally
built as the symbol of the 1929 World Exhibition, it has recently
been renovated by architect Gae Aulenti (who converted the
Gare d'Orsay into one of Paris's foremost museums).

Among the MNAC's numerous treasures is one of the finest
collections of medieval art in the world, divided into Romanesque
and Gothic. The idea for this collection originated in the early 20th
century, when theft of national architectural treasures was rife in
Catalonia. The Romanesque Galleries trace the evolution of Catalan
Romanesque art through a remarkable series of 11th- and 12th-century
murals carefully stripped from the apses of churches throughout
the region, and each painstakingly reconstructed in situ as if they
were still in their original venues. There is also an impressive display
of stone sculptures, wood carvings, gold and silverwork, altar cloths,
enamels and coins. In contrast to the simplicity of the Romanesque
style, the colourful Gothic collection presents over 400 highly ornate
retables and sculptures, including an extraordinary 15th-century
Virgin in full flamenco dress.

The Renaissance and baroque art section includes part of
the dazzling Thyssen-Bornemisza Collection, formerly housed in
Pedralbes Monastery (see page 122), containing predominantly
13th- to 18th-century Italian and German paintings, including
works by Fra Angélico, Titian, Rubens, Canaletto and Velázquez.

The modern art collection is considered the most important
ensemble of Catalan art from the 19th and early 20th centuries.
It starts with works by Marià Fortuny, the earliest of the *Modernistes*

and the first Catalan artist to be widely known abroad, through the less adventurous *Noucentista* (Noucentisme) movement and Impressionism to the avant-garde. There is also a room dedicated exclusively to Pablo Picasso. The sculptures here are especially notable. However, the highlight of the collection is its decorative arts, a magnificent array of jewellery, textiles, stained glass and ceramics by such leading exponents of the era as Cadafalch and Gaudí.

The museum also includes an interesting display of photography, from its origins to the present day, and an important collection of coins, medals and papers from the sixth century BC to the present day. ⓐ Palau Nacional, Montjuïc ⓣ 936 220 376 ⓦ www.mnac.cat ⓛ 10.00–19.00 Tues–Sat, 10.00–14.30 Sun ⓜ Metro: Espanya. Admission charge

RETAIL THERAPY

Considering the number of tourist attractions, Montjuïc is surprisingly devoid of boutiques. However, several museum shops (including CaixaForum, the MNAC and the Fundació Joan Miró) stock a high-quality selection of designer items, books, gifts and arty souvenirs inspired by their collections. In the upper Raval, Carrer Doctor Dou and the surrounding streets have become a new centre of chic, filled with art galleries and fashion boutiques.

Poble Espanyol (Spanish Village)

This purpose-built 'Spanish Village' was originally conceived as a whistle-stop tour of the nation for the 1929 Universal Exposition. The life-sized village contains 117 reproductions of famous or characteristic buildings from all over Spain, many of which now serve as art galleries and artisan workshops selling quality jewellery, wood carvings, leather items, and glass and ceramics, along with more tourist-oriented souvenirs. ➋ Av. del Marquès de Comillas 13, Montjuïc ➊ 933 257 866 Ⓦ www.poble-espanyol.com ⏰ 10.00–18.00 Dec–May; 10.00–20.00 June–Aug; 10.00–19.00 Sept–Nov Ⓜ Metro: Espanya; bus: 13, 50. Admission charge

TAKING A BREAK

Organic £ ➊ Probably the best vegetarian place in town, this refectory-style restaurant has friendly staff, a great all-you-can-eat salad bar, and all the veggie classics. To reach it, walk down Carrer de l'Hospital from La Rambla and take the third left. ➋ C/ Junta de Comerç 11 ➊ 933 010 902 Ⓦ www.antoniaorganickitchen.com ⏰ 12.30–00.00 Ⓜ Metro: Liceu

△ Figs and ametllat, *a traditional Catalan dessert made with almonds*

Soleá £ ❷ A sunny terrace bar on a quiet square with cheery orange décor and international snacks, from tacos to houmous and salad. ⓐ Pl. del Sortidor 14 ❶ 934 410 124 ❸ 12.00–00.00 Tues–Sat, 12.00–16.00 Sun ⓝ Metro: Poble Sec

Oleum ££ ❸ The new restaurant in the MNAC is a heavyweight on Barcelona's serious dining scene, with sweeping views, two Tàpies originals on the walls and an equally stunning menu of intricately presented delights. ⓐ Palau Nacional ❶ 932 890 679 ❸ 13.00–16.00 Tues–Sun ⓝ Metro: Espanya

AFTER DARK

RESTAURANTS

La Bella Napoli £ ❹ This jolly restaurant serves some of the best pizzas in town. ⓐ C/ de Margarit 12 ❶ 934 425 056 ❸ 20.30–00.00 Tues, 13.30–15.45 20.30–00.00 Wed–Sun ⓝ Metro: Paral.lel or Poble Sec

Quimet i Quimet £ ❺ Lined to the ceiling with a tremendous selection of wine, *cava* and spirits, this family-run joint serves some of the finest tapas in town, including preserved seafood and exquisite *montaditos* (snacks on little rounds of bread). ⓐ C/ Poeta Cabanyes 25 ❶ 934 423 142 ❸ 12.00–16.00, 19.00–22.30 Mon–Fri, 12.00–16.00 Sat ⓝ Metro: Paral.lel or Poble Sec

Ca L'Isidre £££ ❻ Despite its downmarket location in Poble Sec, this small bastion of contemporary Mediterranean cuisine counts King Juan Carlos among its regulars. ⓐ C/ Les Flors 12 ❶ 934 411 139 ⓦ www.calisidre.com ❸ 13.30–15.30, 20.30–23.30 Mon–Fri, June–Aug; 13.30–15.30, 20.30–23.30 Mon–Sat, Sept–May ⓝ Metro: Paral.lel

Quo Vadis £££ ❼ Classic Spanish cuisine near the Liceu theatre (see page 65). There's even a special post-theatre menu. ⓐ C/ del Carme 7 ❶ 933 024 072 ⓦ www.restaurantquovadis.com ❶ 13.15–16.00, 20.30–23.30 Mon–Sat ⓝ Metro: Liceu

BARS, CLUBS & LIVE MUSIC

Estadi Olímpic The main venue for mega-star pop concerts, together with neighbouring Palau Sant Jordi. Tickets are best obtained through record shops, but you can also try buying them via the ServiCaixa ATM machines at any branch of the Caixa bank. ⓐ Passeig Olímpic 17 ❶ 934 262 089 ⓝ Bus: 50, 55, 61, 193

Jazz Sí Club The perfect bar for anyone serious about their jazz, with Cuban, rock and blues to boot. Each night is themed on a different genre: check the website for details. ⓐ C/ Requesens 2 ❶ 933 290 020 ⓦ www.tallerdemusics.com ❶ 20.30–23.00 Mon & Wed–Sat, 19.45–22.30 Tues, 18.30–22.00 Sun ⓝ Metro: Sant Antoni. Admission charge

Pastís A tiny rustic bar with a bohemian atmosphere redolent of Paris's Latin Quarter. ⓐ C/ Santa Mònica 4 ❶ 933 187 980 ⓦ www.barpastis.com ❶ 19.30–02.30 Tues–Sun ⓝ Metro: Drassanes

Sala Apolo This lively club, in an elegant old ballroom in the Poble Sec district, caters for all tastes and ages, with African, Latin and Spanish music, live bands and, at weekends, the popular DJ team Nitsa. ⓐ C/ Nou de la Rambla 113 ❶ 934 414 001 ⓦ www.sala-apolo.com ❶ Concerts: 21.00; club: 00.30–06.00 Wed–Sat ⓝ Metro: Paral.lel. Admission charge

La Terrazza Dance till dawn under the stars to house and techno music at this summertime open-air club. ⓐ Poble Espanyol, Av. Marquès de Comillas s/n, Montjuïc ⓘ 932 724 980 ⓦ www.laterrazza.com ⓛ 00.00–06.00 Thur–Sat, May–mid-Oct ⓜ Metro: Espanya; bus: 13, 50

Tinta Roja With its dramatic bordello décor of red velvet and dusty chandeliers this atmospheric bar is the perfect place to enjoy a drink or an offbeat performance of flamenco or jazz on the tiny stage. ⓐ C/ Creu dels Molers 17 ⓘ 934 433 243 ⓦ www.tintaroja.net ⓛ 20.30–02.00 Thur, 20.00–03.00 Fri & Sat, 19.00–01.00 Sun ⓜ Metro: Poble Sec

ENTERTAINMENT

Centre de Cultura Contemporània de Barcelona (CCCB) This arts centre, in a strikingly converted 19th-century workhouse, stages a wide variety of performance arts, including concerts, theatre, dance and film. ⓐ C/ del Montalegre 5 ⓘ 933 064 100 ⓦ www.cccb.org ⓛ 11.00–20.00 Tues, Wed & Fri–Sun, 11.00–22.00 Thur ⓜ Metro: Universitat or Catalunya. Admission charge

Fundació Joan Miró The Joan Miró Foundation (see page 111) contains Spain's chief centre for contemporary music development. It stages frequent concerts including the *Nits de Música* series in June and July. ⓐ Parc de Montjuïc ⓘ 934 439 470 ⓦ www.fundaciomiro-bcn.org ⓜ Metro: Paral.lel then Funicular de Montjuïc; bus: 61

El Tablao de Carmen The flamenco shows here are touristic but fun. Advance booking is essential. ⓐ Poble Espanyol, Montjuïc ⓘ 933 256 895 ⓦ www.tablaodecarmen.com ⓛ Shows: 19.45 & 22.00 Tues–Sun ⓜ Metro: Espanya; bus: 13, 50

Pedralbes, Tibidabo & Les Corts

Pedralbes and Tibidabo are part of Barcelona's Zona Alta (Upper Zone), at a slightly higher elevation than the city centre. These smart hilly suburbs have been popular residential areas for centuries, with beautiful villas, gardens and parks draped over their hillsides. The area also contains some elegant restaurants and bars, but surprisingly few shops.

At 550 m (1,800 ft), Mont Tibidabo, part of the Collserola range, forms the northwestern boundary of Barcelona. Pedralbes is situated at the top of the Avinguda Diagonal to the northwest of the city centre, and contains a beautiful medieval monastery and a Royal Palace with impressive ceramic and decorative arts collections. Immediately south of Pedralbes, the once rural *barri* of Les Corts (The Farmsheds) contains the stadium and museum of FC Barça, Barcelona's remarkable football team.

SIGHTS & ATTRACTIONS

Finca Güell

Every well-to-do member of the Barcelonan middle classes had a *finca* (country house) or a *torre* (villa) in the countryside at the turn of the 20th century and, as a consequence, the Zona Alta area is dotted with fine *Modernista* buildings. One such gem is Finca Güell, former holiday estate of the wealthy Güell family, ardent patrons of Antoni Gaudí. Today the building houses La Càtedra Gaudí, an institution specialising in subjects connected with this famous architect. Although the main buildings are closed to the public, it is still possible to admire his elaborate Moorish-style gatehouses and extraordinary gates depicting a dragon, a veritable

masterpiece of *Modernista* wrought-ironwork. ⓐ Av. de Pedralbes 15
ⓘ 933 177 652 ⓛ 10.50–14.00 Fri–Mon; 25-min guided visits in English:
10.15 & 12.15 Fri–Mon ⓝ Metro: Palau Reial. Admission charge

Monestir de Pedralbes (Pedralbes Monastery)

This exquisite monastery was founded in 1326 by the Catalan King
Jaume II and Queen Elisenda de Montcada for the nuns of the St Clare
of Assisi order. The King died in 1327, just two years after their marriage,
and Queen Elisenda spent the remaining 37 years of her life here. The
Montcadas were among the most powerful families of their day and,
under her auspices, the monastery grew rich and flourished. Today
the monastery is still used by a small community of Clarista nuns.

The monastery takes its name from the Latin *petrae albae* (white
stones), and is best seen in the elegant three-storey cloisters, which
count among the city's finest medieval treasures. Enjoy the tranquillity
of the central courtyard, fragrant with flowers and medicinal herbs,
before visiting the refectory, chapter house, the Queen's grave and
a series of beautifully painted prayer cells. Don't miss the Capella
de Sant Miquel (St Michael's Cell), with its impressive 14th-century
frescoes depicting the life of the Virgin and the Passion. ⓐ Baixada
del Monastir 9 ⓘ 932 562 122 ⓦ www.museuhistoria.bcn.cat
ⓛ 10.00–17.00 Tues–Sat, 10.00–15.00 Sun, Apr–Sept; 10.00–14.00
Mon–Sat, 10.00–15.00 Sun, Oct–Mar ⓝ FGC: Reina Elisenda; bus: 22,
63, 64, 75, 78. Admission charge

Serra de Collserola (Collserola Range)

The hills of the Collserola range lie to the north and west of the
city, forming a wonderful 6,550 ha (16,185 acres) nature reserve
with extensive woodlands full of wildlife and meadows ablaze with
wild flowers. Walking here is easy, as the paths and climbs are well

maintained, with clearly defined picnic areas. This area is best accessed by taking an FGC train to Baixador de Vallvidrera, from where it is a short walk to the information centre, where details of walks and cycle routes are available. Nearby, British architect Norman Foster's glass-and-steel 268 m (879 ft) communications tower, the Torre de Collserola (Collserola Tower), whisks those with a head for heights up to an observation platform by glass-fronted lift for the most sensational views over the city and, on exceptionally clear days, as far as Mallorca. Information centre: ☎ 932 803 552 🕐 09.30–15.00 Ⓝ FGC: Baixador de Vallvidrera

Tibidabo

Tibidabo is the highest peak of the Collserola range and the biggest draw for Barcelonans, who come especially at weekends to enjoy the superb views and the Parc d'Atraccions, an old-fashioned fairground of carousels, bumper cars, a hall of mirrors and a Ferris wheel, combined with a clutch of brand new high-tech attractions. Getting there, on an ancient tram and then by funicular, is all part of a fun family day out. No wonder locals nickname it La Muntanya Màgica (The Magic Mountain). Here too, the Museu d'Autòmats del Tibidabo contains a splendid collection of coin-operated fairground machines dating from the early 20th century. The modern Sagrat

WHAT'S IN A NAME?

The name 'Tibidabo' comes from the words uttered by Satan during his temptation of Christ in the wilderness: '*Haec omnia **tibi dabo*** (all these things will I give to you), *si cadens adoraberis me* (if thou wilt fall down and worship me)'.

Cor (Sacred Heart) crowns the summit of Tibidabo – a neo-Gothic fantasy topped by a massive statue of Christ, visible for miles around. Parc d'Atraccions: ❷ Pl. del Tibidabo 3–4 ❶ 932 117 942 ❿ www.tibidabo.es ❻ 10.00–19.00 or 20.00 late Mar–June & Sept–early Oct; 12.00–22.00 or 23.00 July & Aug; 12.00–18.00 Sat & Sun, mid-Oct–mid-Dec & mid-Jan–late Mar ❿ FGC: Av. Tibidabo, then Tramvia Blau & Funicular de Tibidabo; bus: 194, 195 ❶ Parc d'Atraccions closed mid-Dec–mid-Jan

Tramvia Blau (Blue Tram)

The electric Tramvia Blau is one of the last vestiges of the city's old tram system, in operation since 1902, and a true symbol of Barcelona's identity. Every 20 minutes it rattles along Avingduda Tibidabo between Plaça Kennedy and Plaça Doctor Andreu, passing many fine *Modernista* houses en route. At the end of the journey, take a table on the terrace of La Venta (see page 127). Then, take the **Funicular de Tibidabo** (❶ 932 117 942) from here to the Parc d'Atraccions (see page 123) at Tibidabo's peak. ❻ Tram departs every 20 mins 10.00–20.00 mid-June–mid-Sept; 10.00–18.00 Sat only, mid-Sept–mid-June

CULTURE

Cosmocaixa Barcelona

The city's state-of-the-art science museum is located at the foot of Mont Collserola. It is divided into a number of sections including: the Geological Wall (illustrating Iberian geology); Archimedes Gardens (an open-air space full of hands-on scientific experiments); a Planetarium; a Bubble Planetarium ; and the Flooded Forest (the first living Amazonian rainforest on display inside a science museum). This fascinating new centre is a must for budding scientists: the Toca Toca petting space allows children to encounter animals face to face; Clik (ages three to six) and Flash (ages seven to nine) are areas devoted to scientific experimentation for children. ⓐ C/ Teodor Roviralta 47–51 ☎ 932 126 050 ⓦ www.cosmocaixa.com ⏰ 10.00–20.00 Tues–Sun, mid-Sept–June; 10.00–20.00 July–mid-Sept ⓝ FGC: Av. Tibidabo, then Tramvia Blau & Funicular de Tibidabo; bus: 194, 195. Admission charge

Museu del Futbol Club Barcelona, Camp Nou (Museum of FC Barcelona, Camp Nou)

If you can't get a ticket for a match, at least visit this – one of the city's most popular museums – and stand on the terraces of the second largest football stadium in the world (after Rio's Maracanã), with seating capacity for 120,000 fans. Barcelona is football-crazy and FC Barça is one of Catalonia's flagship institutions. Not only is it the fifth most successful business in Spain, but it is also the richest sports club in the world, with the largest membership of any soccer club.

The museum is under the terraces at Entrance 9, and contains a dazzling display of trophies, strips, photographic archives, audiovisual shows of famous match highlights and an impressive range of memorabilia documenting the history of football from its origins until the present day and, in particular, this club's extraordinary history as a political vehicle and as a rallying point for Catalans. ⓐ Camp Nou football stadium, access 9 ☎ 934 963 600 ⓦ www.fcbarcelona.com ⏰ 10.00–20.00 Mon–Sat, 10.00–14.00 Sun, Apr–Oct; 10.00–18.30 Mon–Sat, 10.00–14.30 Sun, Nov–Mar ⓝ Metro: Collblanc. Admission charge

Palau Reial de Pedralbes (Royal Palace of Pedralbes)

In 1919 the handsome villa of Can Feliu was converted into a royal residence for the King of Spain for the 1929 International Exhibition.

After 1939, it was Franco's city residence and, following a handful of subsequent visits by royalty and heads of state, it was opened to the public in 1960. The impressive state rooms currently contain three museums collectively known as the Disseny Hub (Design Hub), although the planned future location of the Design Hub will be a new purpose-built museum under construction in Glòries.

The Museu de les Arts Decoratives (Museum of Decorative Arts) has an eclectic display of artefacts spanning the early Middle Ages to the present day, with special emphasis on the 20th century, most notably Modernism, Functionalism and Minimalism. The Museu de la Ceràmica (Ceramics Museum) traces Spanish ceramics from the 12th century, arranged by regional styles. The Museu Tèxtil i de la Indumentària (Textile and Clothing Museum) illustrates how the city rose to prosperity during the 1800s thanks to its thriving textile industry, with sumptuous displays of tapestries, textiles, lace, clothing and accessories dating from medieval to modern times. The landscaped grounds make a lovely picnic venue, and there is even a fountain by Gaudí. ⓐ Av. Diagonal 686 ⓣ 932 801 621 ⓦ www.dhub-bcn.cat & www.museuceramica.bcn.cat ⓛ 10.00–18.00 Tues–Sun ⓜ Metro: Palau Reial. Admission charge

RETAIL THERAPY

While Avinguda Diagonal is full of upmarket international fashion and design shops, the upper reaches of this part of town have less to offer in terms of shopping. However, these two shopping centres should cater for most needs:

El Corte Inglés A branch of the city's foremost department store, selling everything from designer fashions to electronics, books, toys, jewellery and cosmetics. There is also a full supermarket, cafeteria and restaurant. ⓐ Av. Diagonal 617 ❶ 933 667 100 ⓦ www.elcorteingles.es ⓛ 10.00–22.00 Mon–Sat ⓝ Metro: Maria Cristina

Pedralbes Centre This shopping centre, next door to El Corte Inglés, contains a wide variety of fashion, shoe, jewellery and design boutiques, including such names as Mango, Timberland and Armani Casa. There are also a handful of eateries and, during winter months, the square outside is turned into an ice rink. ⓐ Av. Diagonal 609–15 ❶ 934 106 821 ⓦ www.pedralbescentre.com ⓛ 10.30–21.00 Mon–Sat ⓝ Metro: Maria Cristina

TAKING A BREAK

La Venta £–££ ❶ This delightful Moorish-style open-air café at the foot of the Tibidabo funicular, with its glass conservatory and outdoor terrace, is the ideal venue for lunch or some light refreshment. ⓐ Pl. Doctor Andreu ❶ 932 126 455 ⓦ www.restaurantelaventa.com ⓛ 13.30–15.15, 21.00–23.15 Mon–Sat ⓝ FGC: Av. Tibidabo, then Tramvia Blau; bus: 194, 195

Merbeyé ££ ❷ An attractive cocktail bar tricked out in red velvet with a sleek terrace in the summer. ⓐ Pl. Doctor Andreu, Tibidabo ❶ 934 179 279 ⓛ 12.00–02.30 Mon–Thur, 12.00–03.30 Fri & Sat, 12.00–02.00 Sun ⓝ FGC: Av. Tibidabo, then Tramvia Blau; bus: 194, 195

AFTER DARK

RESTAURANTS
La Balsa ££ ❸ Enjoy top-notch Catalan, Basque and Mediterranean

cuisine accompanied by bird's-eye views of the city, served atop a circular tower originally built as a water cistern, near the science museum. ⓐ C/ Infanta Isabel 4 ⓣ 932 115 048 ⓦ www.labalsarestaurant.com ⓛ 20.30–23.30 Mon, 13.45–15.30, 20.30–23.30 Tues–Sat, 13.45–15.30 Sun (buffet service only 20.30–23.30 Mon–Sat, Aug) ⓝ FGC: Av. Tibidabo

Neichel £££ ❹ Located at the heart of Pedralbes, this is one of the city's finest restaurants, thanks to Alsace-born chef Jean-Louis Neichel, who boasts the accolade 'the most brilliant ambassador French cuisine has ever had within Spain'. ⓐ C/ Beltran y Rózpide 1–5 ⓣ 932 038 408 ⓦ www.neichel.es ⓛ Lunch & dinner Tues–Sat (reservations required) ⓝ Metro: Palau Reial

BARS, CLUBS & LIVE MUSIC

Elephant Set in a lavishly upholstered mansion, this elegant club has a great summer terrace where the beautiful people of Pedralbes gently bop to mainstream house music. ⓐ Passeig del Til.lers 1 ⓣ 933 340 258 ⓦ www.elephantbcn.com ⓛ 23.30–05.00 Thur–Sat ⓝ Metro: Palau Reial. Admission charge

Mirablau The chic set enjoy this stylish bar and garden terrace on Mont Tibidabo, with its spectacular views over the city and the port. It is especially romantic at dusk when the city lights start to twinkle. ⓐ Pl. Doctor Andreu 1 ⓣ 934 185 879 ⓛ 11.00–04.30 Mon–Thur, 11.00–05.30 Fri–Sun ⓝ FGC: Av. Tibidabo, then Tramvia Blau; bus: 194, 195

---

❶ *Rolling Catalan countryside, Alt Penedès*

OUT OF TOWN
trips

Tarragona & the Costa Daurada

It would be a shame to visit Barcelona without seeing some of the sights of Catalonia, with its beautiful landscapes and wide range of attractions, from wine tasting to rollercoaster rides. To the northwest, the Monestir de Montserrat is one of the most visited sights in Catalonia. South of Barcelona, the Costa Daurada (Golden Coast) is flanked by wide sandy beaches. Along with the popular wine-producing towns of Vilafranca del Penedès and Sant Sadurní d'Anoia, the two main destinations to visit here are Sitges, a delightful resort town that has a huge gay following, and the beautiful city of Tarragona, whose archaeological complex of ancient Roman treasures are a UNESCO World Heritage Site.

GETTING THERE

To get to Sitges, 40 km (25 miles) southwest of Barcelona, take the Renfe train from Passeig de Gràcia, which takes about 45 minutes and leaves you in the centre of town. By car from the city or airport, take the southbound C32 following directions for Castelldelfels-Sitges. A taxi from the airport costs around 50 euros. The Renfe train to Tarragona takes about an hour from Passeig de Gràcia and leaves you two minutes' walk from the foot of the Rambla Nova. By car, drive the A7 motorway southbound, exit number 33 (Tarragona/Valls), which will take you on to the N-240 and then on to Tarragona. For Vilafranca del Penedès, jump on the C4 Renfe Cercanías line from Plaça de Catalunya, which takes 55 minutes. By car, take the A2 motorway southbound.

SIGHTS & ATTRACTIONS

Alt Penedès

Just half an hour's southwest drive from Barcelona, the Alt Penedès is one of Spain's foremost wine-producing areas. Its two main towns, Sant Sadurní d'Anoia and Vilafranca del Penedès, have been producing wine since ancient times.

Vilafranca del Penedès is especially attractive, with beautiful arcaded streets, medieval mansions and an atmospheric Gothic quarter. Here too is the **Vinseum** (❸ Pl. Jaume I 1–3, Vilafranca del Penedès ❶ 938 900 582 ❿ www.vinseum.cat ❸ 10.00–14.00, 16.00–19.00 Tues–Sat, 10.00–14.00 Sun), showing the history and techniques of wine-making in Catalonia. The three main wineries of **Mas Tinell** (❶ 938 170 586 ❿ www.mastinell.com), **Romagosa Torné** (❶ 938 991 353 ❿ www.romagosatorne.com) and **Miguel Torres** (❶ 938 177 400 ❿ www.torres.es), are all located on the outskirts (in the direction of Sant Martí Sarroca), and offer tours and wine tastings (phone for details).

Nearby, Sant Sadurní d'Anoia is the centre of Catalonia's cava industry – producing 90 per cent of Spain's cava – with numerous producers dotted throughout the town. The largest, **Codorníu**

THE LOCAL TIPPLE

The Alt Penedès region produces excellent red (*negre*), white (*blanc*) and rosé (*rosat*) wines as well as *cava*. Look out for *xampanyerías* (champagne bars) serving house cava by the glass, labelled according to quality and sweetness – *brut nature*, *brut*, *sec* and *semi-sec* (the sweetest and cheapest).

(☎ 938 913 342 ⓦ www.codorniu.es 🕐 10.00–16.00 Mon–Thur,
10.00–13.00 Fri–Sun), produces over 40 million bottles a year and
its impressive *Modernista* plant is open to visitors for tours and
tastings with advance booking. Directly opposite the train station,
Freixenet (☎ 938 917 000 ⓦ www.freixenet.es 🕐 09.00–17.00
Mon–Fri, 09.00–13.00 Sat & Sun) is another giant cava producer,
also with tours and tastings with advance booking.
Sant Sadurní d'Anoia Tourist Office ⓐ C/ Hospital 26 ☎ 938 913 188
ⓦ www.turismesantsadurni.com 🕐 10.00–14.00, 16.30–18.30
Tues–Fri, 10.00–14.00 Sat & Sun
Vilafranca del Penedès Tourist Office ⓐ C/ Cort 14 ☎ 938 181 254
ⓦ www.turismevilafranca.com 🕐 16.00–19.00 Mon, 09.00–13.00,
16.00–19.00 Tues–Sat

Beaches

The Costa Daurada takes its name 'Golden Coast' from its broad
sandy beaches and is within easy reach of Barcelona and Tarragona.
Its resorts, including Salou, Altafulla, Torredembarra, Coma-Ruga and
Vilanova i la Geltrú, have a traditional seaside atmosphere and are
hugely popular with families. ⓦ www.costadaurada.info

Montserrat

Montserrat is located 56 km (35 miles) northwest of Barcelona, at the
summit of Catalonia's 1,200 m (4,000 ft) holy mountain (named after
its strangely serrated rock formations: *mont*, mountain; *serrat*, sawtooth).
Dramatically perched at the top of the mountain is Catalonia's most
revered pilgrimage site – the Monestir de Montserrat monastery. Every
year, thousands of worshippers take the thrilling cable-car ride up the
mountain to venerate a small medieval statue of the Madonna and
Child in the church, called *La Moreneta* (The Black Virgin), thought to

have been made by St Luke and brought here by St Peter and discovered in a nearby cave in the 12th century. The statue has been blackened by centuries of smoke from the millions of candles lit in her honour. The monastery museum contains some important paintings by El Greco, Picasso, Dalí and Caravaggio and every day at 13.00 one of Europe's oldest boys' choirs, La Escolania, sings in the church. Take the regular funicular service to the top of the mountains for wonderful walks, hikes and climbs around the various caves and hermitages.

Montserrat Tourist Office ⓐ Pl. de la Creu ⓣ 938 777 777 ⓦ www.montserratvisita.com ⓛ Office: 09.00–20.00 June–Sept; 09.00–18.00 Oct–May; church: 07.30–20.30; museum: 10.00–17.45 Mon–Fri, 10.00–18.45 Sat & Sun

Sitges

Just 40 km (25 miles) south of Barcelona, the attractive beach resort of Sitges has long been a holiday playground of Barcelonans, celebrated for its beautiful Platja d'Or (Golden Beach) that stretches southwards for 5 km (3 miles) from the baroque church of Sant Bartomeu i Santa Tecla. The old town itself is full of bohemian charm, with its narrow streets of flower-bedecked whitewashed cottages, and attractive *Modernista* buildings. From the mid-19th century, Sitges attracted artists and writers, a movement kicked off by *Modernista* painter Santiago Rusinyol, whose villa – Cau Ferrat – is now a must-see museum. The palm-fringed promenade is lined with beach bars, cafés and fish restaurants. However, Sitges is perhaps best known today for its vibrant nightlife. It is also a popular gay holiday destination and comes alive for the outrageous carnival celebrations in February.

Sitges Tourist Office ⓐ C/ Sinia Morera 1 ⓣ 938 944 251 ⓦ www.sitgestur.com ⓛ 09.00–20.00 Mon–Sat, mid-Sept– mid-June; 09.00–14.00, 16.00–18.30 Mon–Sat, mid-June–mid-Sept

Tarragona

Located on a rocky bluff just 97 km (60 miles) southwest of Barcelona, Tarragona boasts the largest ensemble of Roman remains in Spain – the extraordinary architectural legacy of Roman *Tarraco*, former capital of the Iberian peninsula. The Romans captured Tarragona in 218 BC and it became the home of Julius Caesar, and the base for the Roman conquest of Spain. It was also the main commercial centre on this stretch of coast until the 12th century, when Barcelona overshadowed it following the Christian reconquest of the nation.

The Roman remains in the city are remarkable. The **Amfiteatre Romà** (Roman amphitheatre ⓐ Parc del Miracle ❶ 977 242 579 ⌚ 09.00–21.00 Easter–Sept; 09.00–19.00 Oct–Easter) is cut into the hillside overlooking the Mediterranean. This is where the Romans

---

⬇ *The Platja d'Or and church of Sant Bartomeu i Santa Tecla at Sitges*

held their public spectacles, including gladiator fights, before an audience of 12,000 people. During the 12th century, the Romanesque church of Santa Maria del Miracle was built on the site. The **Museu d'Història** (History Museum ❸ Pl. del Rei ❶ 977 236 209 ❿ www.museutgn.com ❹ 09.30–20.30 Tues–Sat, 10.00–14.00 Sun, June–Sept; 09.30–18.00 Tues–Sat, 10.00–14.00 Sun, Oct–May. Admission charge) traces the history of the city through an astonishing array of ancient treasures, while the equally fascinating **Museu Nacional Arqueològic** (National Archaeological Museum ❸ Pl. del Rei 5 ❶ 977 236 209 ❿ www.mnat.es ❹ 09.30–18.00 Mon–Fri, 10.00–14.00 Sat & Sun, Oct–May; 09.30–20.30 Mon–Fri, 10.00–14.00 Sat & Sun, June–Sept. Admission charge) includes a section of the old Roman wall together with busts of emperors, sarcophagi and some beautiful mosaics.

Walk the **Passeig Arqueològic** (Archaeological Promenade ❸ Av. Catalunya ❶ 977 245 796 ❹ 09.00–20.30 Tues–Sat, 09.00–14.30 Sun. Admission charge) around the Roman Walls for excellent views of the city and the hinterland of the Camp de Tarragona. A short walk from the city centre, the **Museu i Necropolis Palaeocristians** (Palaeo-Christian Museum ❸ Passeig de la Independencia 15 ❶ 977 211 175 ❿ www.mnat.es ❹ 10.00–13.30, 16.00–20.00 Tues–Sat, 10.00–14.00 Sun. Admission charge) contains the city's most treasured Roman remains in a former necropolis, with superb mosaics, glass, pottery and ivory.

With so many Roman treasures, it would be easy to overlook Tarragona's mighty **Catedral** (Cathedral ❸ Pl. de la Seu ❶ 977 223 671 ❹ Visiting: 10.00–13.00, 16.00–19.00 Mon–Sat, mid-Mar–May; 10.00–19.00 Mon–Sat, June–mid-Oct; 10.00–17.00 Mon–Sat, mid-Oct–mid-Nov; 10.00–14.00 Mon–Sat, mid-Nov–mid-Mar; also open for Sunday mass. Admission charge for visiting) – a magnificent Romanesque-Gothic construction in the form of a cross, created at the highest point of the city as the centrepiece of the *ciutat vella* (old city).

Tarragona Tourist Office ❷ C/ Major 39 ❶ 977 250 795
🅦 www.tarragonaturisme.cat 🕒 09.00–21.00 Mon–Sat,
10.00–14.00 Sun

Universal Mediterrània Port Aventura

A short distance (67 miles/108 km) south of Barcelona near Tarragona,
Port Aventura is one of Europe's biggest and best theme parks.
Catalonia's answer to Disneyland is an entertaining day out for
all the family, with its exotic shows and fairground rides in themed
Mexican, Chinese, Polynesian, Wild West and Mediterranean settings.
Don't miss the Dragon Khan, Europe's largest rollercoaster with a
stomach-churning eight 360° loops or the Costa Caribe water park.
❷ Port Aventura, signposted from Tarragona or AP-7 motorway
❶ 977 779 090 🅦 www.portaventura.es 🕒 10.00–19.00 Mar–June,
Sept–Oct; 10.00–00.00 July & Aug (check website for other opening
times). Admission charge

🔺 *Tarragona – the atmospheric old city*

Vil.la Casals, Sant Salvador

The celebrated Barcelonan cellist, Pablo Casals (1876–1973), built a summer residence near the beach in the delightful town of Sant Salvador. Today it contains a museum in his honour, documenting the life and work of this musical genius. A veritable child prodigy, he started out on a homemade instrument constructed from a broom handle, a large gourd and some gut strings, and by the age of four he could play the violin, piano, flute and organ. His solo debut in Paris in 1899 launched a touring career that made him famous worldwide. ⓐ Avda Palfuriana 67, Sant Salvador, El Vendrell ⓣ 977 684 276 ⓦ www.paucasals.org ⓛ 10.00–14.00, 16.00–18.00 Tues–Fri, 10.00–14.00, 16.00–19.00 Sat, 10.00–14.00 Sun, mid-Sept–mid-June; 10.00–14.00, 17.00–21.00 Tues–Sat, 10.00–14.00 Sun, mid-June–mid-Sept. Admission charge

RETAIL THERAPY

Shopping here doesn't match Barcelona for choice or style, but Tarragona has some reasonable shops and fashion boutiques, most notably along and around La Rambla Nova and in the Centro Comercial Parc Central on Avinguda Roma. Make sure you stop at a winery in Vilafranca del Penedès or Sant Sadurní di Anoia to stock up your wine cellar.

TAKING A BREAK

Coma-Ruga

Casa Victor £ A popular tapas bar adjoining a smart seafood restaurant on the seafront. ⓐ Passeig Marítim 23 ⓣ 977 681 473 ⓛ 13.00–16.00, 20.00–23.00 Tues–Sat, 13.00–16.00 Sun

Vilafranca del Penedès

Inzolia £ A wine shop and excellent bar specialising, of course, in local wines from Vilafranca. ⓐ C/ Palma 21 ① 938 181 938 ⓦ www.inzolia.com ① 17.00–22.00 Mon, 10.00–14.00, 17.00–22.00 Tues–Sat

AFTER DARK

RESTAURANTS
Montserrat

Abat Cisneros ££ Traditional Catalan specialities in former 16th-century monastery stables. ⓐ Hotel Abat Cisneros, Pl. de Monestir ① 938 777 701 ① 12.45–15.45, 19.45–21.45

Sitges

Mare Nostrum ££ Sophisticated fish restaurant on the seafront. Try the speciality *xató* (escarole salad with salt cod, tuna, anchovies and romesco sauce). ⓐ Passeig de la Ribera 60–2 ① 938 943 393 ⓦ www.restaurantmarenostrum.com ① 13.00–15.30, 20.30–22.30 Thur–Tues ① Closed 15 Dec–1 Feb

Tarragona

Estacio Marítima £££ Top-notch fish restaurant in the atmospheric fishermen's district of Serralló. ⓐ Moll de Costa Tinglado 4 ① 977 232 759 ① 13.00–15.30, 21.00–23.30 Mon–Sat, 13.00–15.30 Sun

Vilafranca del Penedès

Cal Ton ££ Modern minimalist restaurant serving inspiring Catalan cuisine with a twist. ⓐ C/ del Casal 8 ① 938 903 741 ① 13.00–16.00, 20.45–22.30 Wed–Sat, 13.00–16.00 Tues & Sun

NIGHTLIFE

Tarragona has plenty of outdoor cafés and bars in its beach resorts, some with live music. Sitges' most famous street is Carrer Primer de Maig, AKA Sin Street, packed with bars and the main route for carnival. Renowned for its gay scene, there are dozens of gay bars in Carrer Sant Bonaventura alone. **Mediterráneo** (ⓐ C/ Sant Bonaventura 6) is the largest gay disco.

ACCOMMODATION

Montserrat
Abat Cisneros £ A pleasant 3-star hotel with cheap, basic rooms in former monks' cells. ⓐ Pl. de Monestir ⓣ 938 350 201

Sitges
El Xalet £ This small tranquil hotel is housed in a beautiful *Modernista* villa with an outdoor pool and garden. ⓐ C/ Illa de Cuba 33–5 ⓣ 938 110 070 ⓦ www.elxalet.com

Dolce Sitges £££ Stay with the beautiful people at this cutting-edge new 5-star hotel on the outskirts of town. ⓐ Av. Camí de Miralpeix 12 ⓣ 938 109 000 ⓦ www.dolce-sitges-hotel.com

Tarragona
Husa Imperial Tarraco ££ The best hotel in town, with superb views of the coast and the Roman amphitheatre. ⓐ Passeig Palmeres, corner Rambla Vella 2 ⓣ 977 233 040 ⓦ www.husa.es

---

ⓞ *Barcelona's efficient metro network, operated by TMB*

PRACTICAL
information

Directory

GETTING THERE

By air

Barcelona's El Prat de Llobregat Airport (see page 46) is well served by scheduled and low-cost airlines from various UK and European destinations. The airport has four terminals (A, B, C and the new T1 terminal), all linked by a walkway. Foreign airlines mostly use terminal A, while Iberia, the national airline, generally uses terminal B. Terminal T1 will help absorb the increasing number of passengers who arrive at this busy airport.

There are easy connections to the city by bus, train and taxi. As part of a major railway expansion in Barcelona, a new train station will be built nearby, connecting the airport to the Spanish high-speed AVE network, and to lines 2 and 9 of the Barcelona Metro.

The flight time from London is approximately two hours. If you are struggling to find a cheap ticket, it is also worth considering flying with Ryanair, or a charter company such as First Choice Airways, into Girona-Costa Brava airport, which is only 112 km (70 miles) away – just one and a half hours by car or train to Barcelona. Ryanair also flies into Reus, some 100 km (65 miles) south of Barcelona. The best deals can be found by booking well in advance through the websites of leading airlines and tour operators.

British Airways Ⓦ www.britishairways.com

easyJet Ⓦ www.easyjet.com

Iberia Ⓦ www.iberia.com

Ryanair Ⓦ www.ryanair.com

Many people are aware that air travel emits CO_2, which contributes to climate change. You may be interested in the possibility of lessening the environmental impact of your flight through the charity **Climate**

Care (ⓦ www.climatecare.org), which offsets your CO_2 by funding environmental projects around the world.

By rail

RENFE (ⓣ 902 240 202 ⓦ www.renfe.es), the Spanish rail network, links Barcelona to Madrid and other major cities in Spain and abroad. Seat reservations are required on all intercity trains. It takes just 15 hours by train from London via the Channel Tunnel to Barcelona. The monthly *Thomas Cook European Rail Timetable* (ⓣ (UK) 01733 416477; (USA) 1 800 322 3834 ⓦ www.thomascookpublishing.com) has up-to-date schedules for European international and national train services. It's also worth checking out **Rail Europe** (ⓦ www.raileurope.com).

By road

The usual route from the UK by car involves driving down through France and across the Pyrenees to Barcelona. It is advisable to plan your route in advance with a detailed map and to allow at least two days for the journey. Remember to drive on the right, wear your seatbelt at all times and stick to the speed limits: 120 kph (74 mph) on motorways, 100 kph (62 mph) on dual carriageways, 90 kph (56 mph) on other roads, except in urban areas where it is 50 kph (31 mph) unless otherwise stated.

The journey from London to Barcelona by **Eurolines** coach (ⓣ (UK) 08717 818 181; (Barcelona) 932 650 788 ⓦ www.eurolines.es) takes around 26 hours.

By water

The **Port de Barcelona** (ⓣ 902 222 858 ⓣ www.apb.es) is the second-largest cruise centre in the Mediterranean after Athens. There are a total of seven cruise ship terminals (including four at Moll Adossat,

Moll de Sant Bernat, Port Vell by the Maremàgnum shopping centre at the foot of the Ramblas and the North and South terminals), each with tourist information centres, bureaux de change, first aid facilities, car hire, shops, bars and restaurants.

There are regular ferries from the Balearic islands of Mallorca, Menorca and Ibiza, operated by **Trasmediterránea** (☎ 902 454 645 ⓦ www.trasmediterranea.es), as well as a fast ferry service between Palma and Barcelona.

ENTRY FORMALITIES

Citizens of EU countries, USA, Canada, Australia, New Zealand, South Africa and Ireland who hold valid passports do not need a visa to visit Spain for less than 90 days. Other visitors should check with their nearest Spanish consulate.

Visitors to Barcelona from within the EU are entitled to bring their personal effects and goods for personal consumption and not for resale, up to a total of 800 cigarettes and 10 litres of spirits. Duty-free limits for those entering from outside the EU are 200 cigarettes (50 cigars, 250 g tobacco), 1 litre of spirits or 2 litres of wine. No meat or dairy produce is permitted into the country from inside or outside the EU.

MONEY

Spain's currency is the euro, with notes issued in denominations of 5, 10, 20, 50 and 100 euros, and coins of 1 and 2 euros and also 1, 2, 5, 10, 20 and 50 cents. Credit cards are widely used in Barcelona (especially VISA, MasterCard, AMEX and Diners Club) and most UK banks' cash cards can be used to obtain cash in local currency from some ATMs, although the commission charged can be expensive.

HEALTH, SAFETY & CRIME

The water in Barcelona is safe to drink although most people prefer to drink bottled water – either still (*aigua sense gas/agua sin gas*) or carbonated (*aigua amb gas/agua con gas*). A change of diet could lead to stomach upsets, so carry a supply of anti-diarrhoea tablets just in case.

Thanks to a reciprocal healthcare agreement, nationals of EU countries and some other countries can get reduced-price, sometimes free, medical treatment in Spain on presentation of a valid European Health Insurance Card (EHIC). This card gives access to state-provided medical treatment only. Apply online for an EHIC at Ⓦ www.dh.gov.uk and allow at least three weeks to receive the card. On top of this, private medical insurance is still advised and is essential for all other visitors. If you need to consult an English-speaking doctor, ask for help at your hotel reception or call the **Centre Mèdic Assistencial de Catalunya** (ⓐ C/ Provença 281 ❶ 932 153 793 Ⓦ www.centremediccatalonia.com ❶ 08.00–20.00 Mon–Fri); see also page 154 for information on emergency medical aid.

TRAVEL INSURANCE

Whichever mode of transport you choose, make sure you have adequate personal travel insurance for the trip. The policy should give cover for medical expenses, loss, theft, repatriation, personal liability and cancellation expenses. If you are travelling in your own vehicle, you should also check that you are properly insured, and remember to take your driving licence and all relevant insurance documents with you.

Violent crime is rare in Barcelona but the petty crime rate (pick-pocketing, purse-snatching and so on) is high, especially in the Barri Gòtic around La Rambla, Plaça Reial and in El Raval. Don't carry excess cash, and use the hotel safe for valuable goods; don't leave anything visible in a parked car; beware of pickpockets in crowded places (especially on La Rambla); and stick to well-lit populated areas by night. The Guàrdia Urbana (in navy and pale blue uniforms) and increasingly the Mossos d'Esquadra (in navy and light blue uniforms with a red trim) keep law and order in the city and are generally helpful in minor cases of crime and security. If you need a police station, ask for *la comisaria*. (See also page 155 for information on emergency police assistance.)

OPENING HOURS

Business hours in Barcelona are generally 08.00 or 09.00–18.00 or 19.00 Monday to Friday, with a long lunch break and siesta from 13.30 until 15.30 or 16.00. Most banks open 08.30–14.00 Monday to Friday but do not close for lunch in the city. Some main branches also open 08.30–12.30 on Saturdays.

Museum hours vary, but as a general rule museums are closed on Sunday afternoons and all day Monday. Some of the smaller museums close for the lunchtime siesta.

Large shops and chains open from 10.00 to 20.00 or 21.00 Monday to Saturday. Smaller or independent shops open and close around the same time, but take a lunch break from 13.30 or 14.00 until 16.30 or 17.00. On Sundays all shops are closed except for bakeries, which are open in the morning, kiosks and shops in licensed tourist zones such as the Maremàgnum shopping centre and La Rambla. Market times vary, but the city's food markets (including La Boqueria) are generally open every morning Monday to Saturday.

LANGUAGE

Barcelona is a bilingual city with two official languages, Catalan and (Castilian) Spanish. Catalan is not a dialect but a distinct language with a long and proud history. It is spoken by over six million people and understood by 11 million (in Catalonia, Valencia, the Balearic islands, Roussillon in southern France, Andorra, and Alghero in Sardinia). Most Barcelonans are bilingual and switch back and forth between Catalan and Spanish depending on who they are talking to.

Most hotels, museum and tourist office staff will speak some English but any attempt to speak Spanish, rather than English, will go down well. However, if you can manage a few words of Catalan, you'll really win people over.

TOILETS

With the exception of the most central beaches, it is difficult to find public toilets in the city, so you are best advised to rely on the facilities provided in museums, galleries, shops, bars and restaurants, which are usually free.

CHILDREN

Children receive a warm welcome in Barcelona, and they are welcomed rather than tolerated in cafés, restaurants and even bars although very few restaurants offer specific children's menus. Nappies, baby food and formula milk can be bought from supermarkets and pharmacies but, if you have a preferred brand take a supply with you. If you need to hire a car seat for a child, double-check availability when making the booking and also check the seat carefully before fitting. Ask your hotel reception about babysitters and local crèches. Some hotels offer a baby-listening service for the evenings.

There are great parks and playgrounds for children to enjoy throughout the city, and lovely sandy beaches (see page 74) equipped with playgrounds, shops, showers and lifeguards. At Nova Mar Bella, there are small boats for hire in summer. Many of the museums and attractions also appeal to children, such as L'Aquàrium (see page 72) with its hands-on exhibits and fascinating underwater tunnel, the exciting Cosmocaixa science museum and planetarium (see page 124) and the state-of-the-art Museu d'Història de Catalunya (see page 79) with loads of interactive sections.

Older children may find the modern art installations in the MACBA (see page 112) amusing, and if your kids have a sweet tooth you should treat them to a trip to the Museu Xocolata (Chocolate Museum, see page 80). The Museu Marítim (see page 112) has boats which children can climb aboard in order to get a little taste of life at sea. Budding footballers will love visiting the Camp Nou (see page 125), one of the world's biggest football stadiums and home to FC Barça.

There are several places where you can have good old-fashioned theme park fun, like the Port Aventura (see page 137) just south of Tarragona, one of Europe's largest theme parks. Closer to the centre and slightly more tame, try the Parc d'Atraccions on Tibidabo (see page 123); the city zoo (see page 77) also appeals to children young and old. La Font Màgica (see page 109) offers a spectacular sound-and-light extravaganza based around a huge fountain.

If you're on a budget, there are plenty of parks in Barcelona. One not to miss is the Parc de la Ciutadella (see page 77), a boating lake with a life-size elephant statue. A simple walk up La Rambla (see page 63) will keep kids amused with all the street entertainments on offer. Even some of the city's transportation modes are fun, especially the cable cars and funiculars. For a real treat, Las Golondrinas (see page 77) offer boat trips around the harbour and to the Olympic port.

COMMUNICATIONS

Internet

Barcelona is one giant Wi-Fi spot, with over 500 municipal spaces including libraries, cultural centres, the airport, municipal markets and museums offering wireless internet access. Hotels and hostels often offer broadband internet, and cybercafés are dotted around the city. Try:

Abre Barcelona ⓐ Aribau 308 ⓣ 932 020 274 Ⓦ www.abrebarcelona.com
ⓛ 09.00–23.30 Mon–Fri, 12.00–23.30 Sat & Sun

Bornet ⓐ Barra de Ferro 3, in front of Picasso Museum ⓣ 932 681 507
Ⓦ www.bornet-bcn.com ⓛ 10.00–23.00 Mon–Fri, 12.00–23.00 Sat & Sun

Verdi Click ⓐ C/ Verdi 9, Gràcia ⓣ 934 158 839 ⓛ 09.30–22.00 Mon–Fri,
10.00–14.00, 16.00–22.00 Sat, 16.00–22.00 Sun

TELEPHONING SPAIN

To phone Spain from abroad, dial the international access code (00) followed by the country code 34. All telephone numbers in Barcelona begin with 93 followed by a seven-digit number.

TELEPHONING ABROAD

To phone home from Barcelona, dial the international access code (00) followed by the relevant country code: UK 44, USA and Canada 1, Australia 61, New Zealand 64, Republic of Ireland 353, South Africa 72, then the local code (minus the initial 0) and finally the number you want.

Phone

Public phones take coins, phone cards and credit cards, and have instructions for use in English. You can buy phone cards from post offices and tobacconists. Spain has an excellent mobile phone network. The **Páginas Amarillas** (Yellow Pages Ⓦ www.paginasamarillas.es) is a useful source for telephone numbers.

International enquiries 🕿 11825
National enquiries 🕿 11818
Operator 🕿 1002

Post

The Spanish postal service **Correos** (Ⓦ www.correos.es) is efficient and its bright yellow offices and post boxes are easy to spot. Take a numbered ticket from the machines by the entrance and wait for your turn. Stamps (*sellos*) can be purchased at post offices and tobacconists.

Central post office ⓐ Plaça Antonio López, Barri Gòtic 🕿 934 868 050 🕘 08.30–21.00 Mon–Fri, 08.30–14.00 Sat

ELECTRICITY

Electricity is supplied at 220 volts, 50 Hz. Spanish plugs are of the two-pin round plug variety, so an adapter will be required for British and non-Continental appliances. US and other visitors with 110-volt appliances will need to use a voltage transformer too.

TRAVELLERS WITH DISABILITIES

Compared to many major cities, disabled access in Barcelona is very good and continually being improved. Most of the city's modern attractions (such as MACBA and Cosmocaixa), along with many buses and metro stations, have good access for those with disabilities.

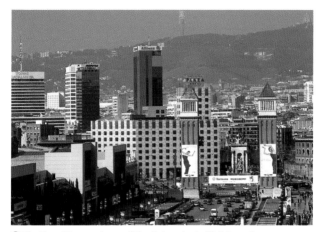

⬥ The Plaça d'Espanya is one of the city's major traffic intersections

Metro stations with lifts and level-entry platforms are marked with a wheelchair symbol on the Barcelona Metro official transport map. However, in the narrow streets and ancient buildings of the historic centre and in some of the Modernista houses, access is poor.

The best source of information and advice on access in Barcelona is **Accessible Barcelona** (ⓣ 934 566 135 ⓦ www.accessiblebarcelona.com), run by English-born wheelchair user Craig Grimes as part of a bigger project **Accessible.travel** (ⓦ www.accessible.travel). The company can reserve guaranteed accessible hotel rooms as well as transfers and other specialist equipment.

TOURIST INFORMATION

Barcelona's Tourist Information Offices (Turisme de Barcelona) are useful for maps, accommodation, attractions and event information and any other queries you have about the city. There are several branches:

Airport @ Terminals A & B 🕐 09.00–21.00

Plaça de Catalunya @ Pl. de Catalunya, underground opposite
El Corte Inglés 🕐 09.00–21.00

Plaça Sant Jaume @ C/ Ciutat 2 🕐 09.00–20.00 Mon–Fri,
10.00–20.00 Sat, 10.00–14.00 Sun

Sants Railway Station @ Pl. Països Catalans 🕐 08.00–20.00 summer;
08.00–20.00 Mon–Fri, 08.00–14.00 Sat & Sun, winter

There are also a number of information booths at strategic
points around the city:

Columbus Monument @ Pl. Portal de la Pau 🕐 09.00–21.00

Estació del Nord @ C/ Alí Bei 80 🕐 09.30–14.30 Mon–Sat

Plaça Espanya @ Av. Maria Cristina/Pl Espanya 🕐 10.00–20.00 July–Sept;
10.00–16.00 Oct–June

Sagrada Família @ C/ Sardenya (in front of the Passion façade)
🕐 10.00–20.00 July–Sept; 10.00–16.00 Oct–June

The tourist office also has a multilingual call centre for general
tourist information 🕿 807 117 222 (from Spain); 932 853 834 (from
abroad). Its official website, together with the Spanish National
Tourist Office, provides further details (in English, French, Spanish
and Catalan) about the city and the region, its history, events
and facilities.

Spanish National Tourist Office Ⓦ www.spain.info

Turisme de Barcelona Ⓦ www.barcelonaturisme.com

For further information on the city's acclaimed *Modernista*
architecture and the Ruta del Modernisme (a self-guided walking
route past many of the city's Modernist highlights), contact the
Centre del Modernisme desk in the Plaça de Catalunya tourist
office (see above).

BACKGROUND READING

An Olympic Death, Manuel Vázquez Montalbán. Crime novel, written just before the 1992 Olympics, with a Barcelona native as the central detective character.

Barcelona Design Guide, Juliet Pomés Leiz & Ricardo Feriche. A comprehensive guide to Barcelona's 'designer' culture.

Barcelona: The Great Enchantress, Robert Hughes. A 21st-century portrait of the city.

Barcelonas, Manuel Vázquez Montalbán. Reflections on the city by one of its most prominent modern authors.

The Best of Worlds, Quim Monzo. Black humour with Barcelona as its backdrop, by Catalonia's best-selling author.

Homage to Barcelona, Colm Tóibín. A fascinating account of the city, its art and architecture.

Homage to Catalonia, George Orwell. First-hand observations of life in the region during the Spanish Civil War.

The Shadow of the Wind, Carlos Ruiz Zafón. This mystery story set in 1950s Barcelona was a runaway bestseller.

The Time of the Doves, Merce Rodoreda. Novel set in the city during the Civil War, by one of Catalonia's most celebrated women writers.

Emergencies

EMERGENCY NUMBERS

Ambulance ❶ 061

Fire ❶ 080

Guardia Urbana (City police) ❶ 092

Mossos d'Esquadra (Emergencies and traffic accidents) ❶ 088

Policía Nacional (National police) ❶ 091

RACC (Breakdown service) Av. Diagonal 687 ❶ 934 955 050

Ⓦ www.racc.es

To call any emergency service from a mobile phone, dial ❶ 112

MEDICAL SERVICES

Should you become seriously ill, lists of local doctors (*medicos*), dentists (*dentistas*) and hospitals can be found in telephone directories or by contacting your consulate, who will have lists of English-speaking practitioners. Alternatively, ask your hotel reception to help or, in a real emergency, dial 061 for an ambulance. If you have a valid European

---

EMERGENCY PHRASES

Help!	**Fire!**	**Stop!**
¡Socorro!	¡Fuego!	¡Stop!
¡Sawkoro!	*¡Fwegoh!*	*¡Stop!*

Call the police/fire service/ambulance!
Llame la policía/los bomberos/una ambulancia!
Lyameh la polithia/los bombehros/una amboolanthia!

Health Insurance Card (EHIC, see page 145), you should ensure that the doctor is part of the Spanish healthcare system as the card covers only state-provided medical treatment.

Pharmacies (*farmàcias*) are widespread, and their highly trained staff can provide medical advice and over-the-counter drugs. In an emergency, go straight to the city centre casualty department, **Centre d'Urgències Perecamps** (ⓐ Av. de les Drassanes 13–15 ☎ 934 410 600 Ⓜ Metro: Drassanes).

POLICE

There are several police stations throughout the city including:

Barceloneta ⓐ Passeig Joan de Borbó 32 ☎ 932 240 600

Eixample ⓐ C/ de Guadalajara 3 ☎ 932 903 021

El Raval ⓐ C/ Nou de la Rambla 78–80 ☎ 932 902 844

There is also a multilingual police service at the Guardia Urbana station on La Rambla near Plaça Reial.

Guardia Urbana de Ciutat Vella ⓐ La Rambla 43 ☎ 932 562 430

EMBASSIES & CONSULATES

Australian ⓐ Pl Gal.la Placídia 1, Barcelona ☎ 924 909 013

British ⓐ Av. Diagonal 477 (13th floor), Barcelona ☎ 933 666 200

Canadian ⓐ C/ Elisenda de Pinós 10, Barcelona ☎ 932 042 700

Irish ⓐ Gran Via Carles III (10th floor), Barcelona ☎ 934 915 021

New Zealand ⓐ Travessera de Gràcia 64 (2nd floor), Barcelona ☎ 932 090 399

South African ⓐ C/ Claudio Coello 91, Madrid ☎ 91 436 3780

United States ⓐ Passeig Reina Elisenda 23, Barcelona ☎ 932 802 227

Editorial/project management: Lisa Plumridge
Copy editor: Monica Guy
Layout/DTP: Alison Rayner

The publishers would like to thank the following individuals and organisations for supplying the copyright photographs for this book: Kirsten Foster, pages 32, 38–9, 87 & 141; Victor Puig, pages 16, 22, 40, 63 & 67; Eva Serrabassa/iStockphoto.com, pages 46–7; Pedro Valdeolmillos, page 116; Teresa Fisher, all others.

Send your thoughts to
books@thomascook.com

- **Found a great bar, club, shop or must-see sight that we don't feature?**
- **Like to tip us off about any information that needs a little updating?**
- **Want to tell us what you love about this handy little guidebook and more importantly how we can make it even handier?**

Then here's your chance to tell all! Send us ideas, discoveries and recommendations today and then look out for your valuable input in the next edition of this title.

Email the above address (stating the title) or write to: pocket guides Series Editor, Thomas Cook Publishing, PO Box 227, Coningsby Road, Peterborough PE3 8SB, UK.

WHAT'S IN YOUR GUIDEBOOK?

Independent authors Impartial up-to-date information from our travel experts who meticulously source local knowledge.

Experience Thomas Cook's 165 years in the travel industry and guidebook publishing enriches every word with expertise you can trust.

Travel know-how Thomas Cook has thousands of staff working around the globe, all living and breathing travel.

Editors Travel-publishing professionals, pulling everything together to craft a perfect blend of words, pictures, maps and design.

You, the traveller We deliver a practical, no-nonsense approach to information, geared to how you really use it.

Useful phrases

English	Catalan/*pronunciation*	Spanish/*pronunciation*
BASICS		
Yes	Si/*Si*	Si/*Si*
No	No/*Noh*	No/*Noh*
Please	Si us plau/*Seeus plow*	Por favor/*Por fabor*
Thank you	Gràcies/*Graseeas*	Gracias/*Gratheeas*
Hello	Hola/*Ola*	Hola/*Ola*
Goodbye	Adéu/*Ade-u*	Adiós/*Adeeos*
Excuse me/Sorry	Perdoni/*Perdonee*	Perdone/*Perdoneh*
That's okay	D'acord/*Dacort*	De acuerdo/*De akwerdo*
I don't speak Catalan/Spanish	No parlo català/*Noh parlu catalah*	No hablo español/*Noh ahblo espanyol*
Do you speak English?	Parla anglès?/*Parla angless?*	¿Habla inglés?/*Ahbla eengless?*
Good morning	Bon dia/*Bon diya*	Buenos días/*Bwenos dee-ahs*
Good afternoon/evening	Bona tarda/*Bona tardah*	Buenas tardes/*Bwenos tarrdess*
Goodnight	Bona nit/*Bona nit*	Buenas noches/*Bwenos notchess*
My name is ...	El meu nom es.../*El me-o nom es...*	Me llamo.../*Me yamo...*
NUMBERS		
One	U (un, una)/*U (un, unah)*	Uno/*Oono*
Two	Dos/*Dos*	Dos/*Dos*
Three	Tres/*Tres*	Tres/*Tres*
Four	Quatre/*Cwatra*	Cuatro/*Cwatro*
Five	Cinc/*Sinc*	Cinco/*Thinco*
Six	Sis/*Sis*	Seis/*Seys*
Seven	Set/*Set*	Siete/*Seeyetey*
Eight	Vuit/*Vweet*	Ocho/*Ocho*
Nine	Nou/*Now*	Nueve/*Nwebey*
Ten	Deu/*Deyu*	Diez/*Deeyeth*
Twenty	Vint/*Vint*	Veinte/*Beintey*
Fifty	Cinquanta/*Sincwanta*	Cincuenta/*Thincwenta*
One hundred	Cent/*Sent*	Cien/*Thien*
SIGNS & NOTICES		
Airport	Aeroport/*Ayroport*	Aeropuerto/*Ayropooehrto*
Railway station	Estació de trens/*Estaseeoh de trens*	Estación de trenes/*Estatheeon de trenes*
Platform	Plataforma/*Plataforma*	Andén/*Anden*
Smoking/Non-smoking	Fumar/Prohibit fumar/*Foomar/Prooeebeet foomar*	Fumar/Prohibido fumar/*Foomar/Proeebeedo foomar*
Toilets	Lavabos/*Lababos*	Lavabos/*Lababos*
Ladies/Gentlemen	Senyores/Senyors/*Senyores/Senyors*	Señoras/Señores/*Senyoras/Senyores*
Metro/Tram/Bus	Metro/Tranvia/Autobús/*Metro/Tranbiya/Awtoeboos*	Metro/Tramvia/Autobús/*Metro/Trambiya/Awtoeboos*